# DATE DUE

| | | | |
|---|---|---|---|
| | | | |
| | | | |
| | | | |
| | | | |
| | | | |
| | | | |
| | | | |
| | | | |
| | | | |
| | | | |
| | | | |
| | | | |
| | | | |
| | | | |
| | | | |
| | | | |
| | | | |
| | | | |
| | | | |
| | | | |
| | | | |

JOSTEN'S   30 508

D1502762

# Concepts in Modern Educational Dance

**THE HUMAN MOVEMENT SERIES**
General Editor: Dr. H.T.A. Whiting

**HUMAN MOVEMENT: a field of study.**

*Edited by: J.D. BROOKE and H.T.A. WHITING*


**Readings in the Aesthetics of Sport.**


*Edited by: H.T.A. WHITING*


**Personality in a Physical Education Context.**

*By: H.T.A. WHITING, K. HARDMAN, L.B. HENDRY and MARILYN G. JONES*


**Readings in Sports Psychology.**

*Edited by: H.T.A. WHITING*


**Techniques for the Analysis of Human Movement.**

*By D.N. GRIEVE, DORIS MILLER, D.L. MITCHELSON, J. PAUL & A.J. SMITH*

**Educational Gymnastics Themes.**

*By: JEAN WILLIAMS*


**Proprioceptive Control of Human Movement.**

*By: J. DICKINSON*

# Concepts in Modern Educational Dance

by H.B. REDFERN

M.Ed., Dip.Phil., Diploma of the Art
of Movement Studio, Surrey.
Formerly Principal Lecturer in Dance
and Physical Education, Crewe College
of Eduction, and Visiting Lecturer in
the Speech and Drama Department,
University of Natal. At present
free-lance lecturer in Dance and
Education, specialising in Aesthetics.

**Henry Kimpton Publishers**
**London 1973**

Standard Book Number 85313 772-2


Computerised origination by Autoset, Brentwood.
Printed by Unwin Bros. Ltd., Woking.

# List of Contents

Editor's Foreword VI

Preface VII

Acknowledgements VIII

Introduction IX

A  Imagination 1

B  Effort (Part I) 25
   Effort (Part II) 41

C  Modern Educational Dance 61
   (1) "Free" aspects 65
   (2) a. "Expressive" aspects 71
   (2) b. "Impressive" aspects 87
   (3) Social aspects 105
   (4) Principles of movement 117

Index of Proper Names 147
Subject Index. 149

# EDITOR'S FOREWORD

The introduction of a series of books with the common theme of Human Movement has been precipitated by the current interest in Human Movement Studies being shown in universities and colleges of education throughout the world. While in the past such studies have been nurtured under the umbrella term 'physical education', this should not lead to the belief that the study of physical education and the study of human movement are in the same logical category. Physical education theory as part of educational theory is concerned with educational processes in which motor activity predominates. Human Movement Studies on the other hand are not tied to any practical functions. This is not to deny that many of the areas outlined in the series source text* may be of fundamental interest to students of physical education, but cautions against its limitation to a particular group of professional people or to the necessity to make it an applied study.

Laban's studies of human movement have had considerable impact on the teaching of physical education in schools and colleges of education but such principles as have been established have rarely been subjected to scientific or logical analysis. Only recently have questions begun to be asked about the nature of the subject and interpretations which have been put on Laban's work. As in other educational systems, practice has preceded critical analysis. In the present contribution to the Human Movement series, Betty Redfern brings her philosophical expertise and practical knowledge as an educationist with a particular interest in the arts and in physical education to bear on the interpretation of Laban's work and its implications for teaching. In so doing, she provides a reasoned account of his theories with particular reference to dance.

H.T.A. Whiting
Series Editor

BROOKE J.D. & WHITING H.T.A. (Eds.) (1972). "Human Movement—a field of study". London: Henry Kimpton.

# PREFACE

These essays are extended versions of papers originally given in the University of London within a series of philosophy lectures for the B. Ed. syllabus ("B") in Physical Education, which is concerned chiefly with movement as a medium of expression and communication.

Since educational theory is now established as an interdisciplinary study of which philosophy is an integral part, and in view of the place which the latter has in both the three-year Certificate of Education and B. Ed. courses, it was assumed that students were already familiar with modern analytical techniques and with the tenor of current philosophical debate about a variety of topics including, of course, the concept of education itself. However, although this volume is intended primarily for students and teachers engaged in the study to degree level of education and movement, particularly dance, it is hoped that it may also prove of interest and value to others, even if they lack acquaintance with the nature of philosophical inquiry.

Contrary to the widespread view first expressed by Wittgenstein (1953) that "philosophy leaves everything as it is," it is becoming increasingly felt, not least in the field of education, that it can and does have, in fact, an important bearing on practical matters. While, therefore, not finding teaching material or questions of presentation discussed in these pages, anyone having responsibility for the subject variously known as "modern educational dance," "creative dance," or "the art of movement" (among others), might nevertheless be prepared to consider modifying both his aims and the content and methods of his teaching as a result of pondering some of the issues herein raised.

Although a common thread may be detected in all three studies, since the overall concern is with the claim of dance to be regarded as an educational activity, this is essentially a collection of essays which may be taken in any order, rather than a uniform book. On the other hand, some advantage might be gained from reading them in the sequence presented, inasmuch as the first takes a general concept, that of *imagination,* which has merited considerable attention from philosophers (though not, as far as is known, specifically in relation to movement or dance) and which serves more readily as an introduction to what is involved in philosophical inquiry; whereas the other two deal with more technical concepts peculiar to "art of movement." The last concentrates on the whole notion of *modern educational dance,* with particular reference to the exposition of this by Rudolf Laban, and is preceded by an examination of *effort* and associated ideas, on which the former account will be shown largely to depend.

# ACKNOWLEDGEMENTS

I wish to thank the many friends who have urged me to publish these lectures and who have given me constant encouragement throughout. In particular I am grateful to Mrs. Sonia Greger, Senior Lecturer in Philosophy, Crewe College of Education, and Miss June Layson, Lecturer in the Department of Physical Education, University of Leeds, who from time to time have read and discussed with me various parts of the script.

I owe a special debt of gratitude to Mr. Peter Renshaw, Lecturer in Education, University of Leeds Institute of Education, not only for his penetrating comments on the first two chapters, but also for his philosophical stimulus during the period when we were colleagues at Wall Hall College of Education. Thanks are also due to Mr. Gordon Curl, Principal Lecturer in Physical Education, for his careful reading of parts of the last chapter, and for a refreshing exchange of views in this connection.

Finally, it would be imposssible for me to attempt to say anything at all about modern educational dance without acknowledging the inspiration and guidance over the years of Miss Lisa Ullmann, Director of the Art of Movement Studio, Addlestone, Surrey, who, while not directly connected with the publication of this volume, has always borne my questioning with patience and tolerance, and has given generously of her time in helping me to seek answers.

None of these, however, necessarily shares the views expressed, and any errors remain entirely my responsibility.

H.B. Redfern,
October, 1971.

# INTRODUCTION

However firmly we believe that what we teach in schools and colleges is educationally worthwhile, and however strong our convictions as to the value of the procedures we adopt, we are failing in our task if we remain unready or unwilling to reconsider and reassess from time to time, as carefully and dispassionately as possible, the theory which underpins our practice. To paraphrase a famous saying of Socrates, "A subject unexamined is not worth pursuing."

In such an enterprise philosophy has a most important part to play. This is not because it is "a sort of superior and profounder science," as O'Connor (1957) has put it, which can "be expected to answer difficult and important questions about human life and man's place and prospects in the universe," but because it is, rather, "an activity of criticism and clarification." Not only is it of assistance, however, in attempts to discern problems of meaning, to make clear what it is we are talking about, and to reveal assumptions and presuppositions which may underlie what we and others say; but also, in its concern with the nature of knowledge it is pertinent to questions of curriculum construction and to the business of providing arguments and justifications for the inclusion of particular subjects.

In the field of "movement" and dance, what seem to be in considerable need of objective examination and critical evaluation at the present time are the theories[*] and ideas of Rudolf Laban. Although there seems to be, as Curl (1969) points out, "an ever-widening gap between the underlying philosophy and the practice of Laban's work," much that is carried on in this area in schools and colleges derives from his teachings, and it is with some of his concepts that two essays in this book are mainly concerned. These and associated topics have been the centre of controversy among physical educationists and others for a number of years, especially inasmuch as they are bound up with problems regarding the nature of "art of movement," what constitutes its boundaries, and its relationship with other subjects. As Curl also remarks, ". . . research into theoretical foundations has not

---

[*] The terms "theories" and "theory" are used throughout in relation to Laban in the broad sense of "speculations" or "hypotheses" and not in the strict scientific sense.

been a strong characteristic of movement education; teaching has largely rested on a sensitive and intuitive approach: . ."

The debate has not been illuminated by the tendency of many to adopt an "either/or" approach, to be either "for" or "against" Laban. But there is no need (indeed it is a thorough over-simplification of the matter and to our positive disadvantage) to think in terms of accepting or rejecting *in toto* a theoretical structure which, though suffering from a variety of confusions, affords the sort of basis essential to the study and practice of what ultimately must be recognised as an *aesthetic form of understanding,* * and as such, worthy of consideration in education. Laban is not the first whose underlying rationale falls somewhat short of the practice he inspired; moreover his pronouncements on education, no less than his speculations concerning movement, are to be judged by different standards today in the light of more recent inquiries, conceptual as well as empirical, into these subjects.

Nevertheless, as has been said of Freud:-

> His theoretical work has a kind of creative untidiness about it. He never presents us with a finished structure but with the far more exciting prospect of working through a number of possible ways of talking and thinking. One result of this is that his conceptual errors and unclarities are usually far more interesting and suggestive than the careful precision with which so many writers . . . equip themselves . . . (MacIntyre, 1958).

Some of Laban's ideas (which in fact might prove eventually to be among his most fruitful, such as the notion of "shadow movements," for example), remain undeveloped or receive only scant treatment in his published writings, often being nothing more than the subject of brief and rather arbitrary statements. And it is not always clear whether apparent contradictions are due to basic inconsistencies in his thinking, or to modifications and changes in his views which became necessary as these were further explored, but which he failed to make explicit in any neatly rounded-off reformulation of his theories.

In addition, however (and quite apart from the difficulties presented by writing in a foreign language, and by the very nature of the ideas themselves in respect of verbal expression), Laban is apt to make little distinction between what are matters of opinion and what are matters of fact—or, at least, verifiable in principle. Many of his claims and assertions lack either empirical confirmation or rational justification and (as in the case of human behaviour in general), a good deal of the knowledge

---

* For the significance of this phrase here and throughout, see Hirst (1966), and of the related one, "modes of experience," see Hirst & Peters (1970). It is also possible that some of Laban's ideas are relevant in education in respect of *personal and interpersonal understanding,* and in connection with studies in the field of non-verbal communication and personality assessment (see Essay C, section 3, below).

relevant to the kinds of questions that he was in effect posing awaits further discoveries from, for example, neurophysiology, psychology, anthropology, and other related disciplines. While such investigations are not of a philosophical nature, what *is* within the scope of philosophy is to distinguish between those issues which require empirical evidence and those which are not to be settled by any amount of scientific research, but demand conceptual clarification.

What is therefore necessary in this connection is that Laban's theories are subjected to careful sifting so that problems of meaning be elucidated, certain ideas reinterpreted and, as far as education is concerned, claims for the inclusion of dance in the curriculum which do have some validity separated out from those which are erroneous or irrelevant. None of the essays in this volume should, however, be regarded as more than a preliminary attempt to clear the ground for a fuller investigation of these and other topics. If, therefore, they prompt others to present counter-arguments, this cannot but be to the good; and if what is said is thought to misrepresent or misinterpret Laban, this opens up opportunities for those who have clearer insight to correct such misapprehensions and to explain his theories in greater detail. But it need hardly be said that the project would not have been undertaken in the first place were I not assured of the importance for education of some of his work, and of the need for this to be justly evaluated both to promote more enlightened discussion of the claim of dance to be an educational activity, and to help rationalise the present confused situation in respect of "art of movement."

If there are some who, caught up in the fashionable anti-intellectual ferment of our time, and the almost anti-vivisectionist attitude towards analysis which seems to accompany it, are apt to recoil in horror at the mere mention of such an exercise, it might be worth reminding them that Laban himself claimed to stand for mobility as much in the sphere of thinking as of movement, and was himself always open to fresh perspectives. Excursions into philosophy are notoriously disturbing—but not all disturbing experiences are unrewarding, nor indeed unpleasant; and whatever else "movement" may mean, it *must* mean not remaining in the same position.

Should these studies do no more than rouse people to consider whether they ought to adopt a new stance, to look again at what Laban actually says, and to rethink the grounds on which they either accept or reject particular aspects of his teachings, they will not have failed completely. And they will have far exceeded the original intentions of the author if they encourage any to take further steps to ensure that they recognise a philosophical problem when they meet one which, in O'Connor's (1957) words, is "to be safeguarded against one of the commonest and most dangerous of intellectual errors—that of talking philosophy unawares."*

In coming to recognise the doubtful nature of many beliefs to which in the past I

---

* A variety of sources is referred to throughout which it is hoped may be of value for further study.

myself have uncritically subscribed, I take comfort in the fact that others too, including many of eminence, are sometimes obliged to revise their former pronouncements and relinquish long-cherished assumptions. In particular the words of Ryle, at the close of his Introduction to *The Concept of Mind* (1949), are all too apt, but in this case, because of the urgency of the present situation, his final remarks there would be reversed to read:-

> Primarily I hope to help other theorists to recognise our malady and to benefit from my medicine. Only secondarily am I trying to get some disorders out of my own system.

### References

CURL G.F. (1969) Philosophic foundations (Part 6). *L.A.M.G.Mag.* **43**, 27-44.
HIRST P.H. (1966) Educational theory. In J.W. Tibble (Ed.) "The Study of Education". London: Routledge & Kegan Paul.
HIRST P.H. & PETERS R.S. (1970) "The Logic of Education". London: Routledge & Kegan Paul.
MACINTYRE A.C. (1958) "The Unconscious". London: Routledge & Kegan Paul.
O'CONNOR D.J. (1957) "An Introduction to the Philosophy of Education". London: Routledge & Kegan Paul.
RYLE G. (1949) "The Concept of Mind". London: Hutchinson.

# A

# IMAGINATION

# A IMAGINATION

In education generally, but among advocates of arts subjects in particular, there is a good deal of talk of the importance of imaginative activity and of developing the imagination. The latter may even be an avowed aim, and to be lacking in imagination is apt to be universally deplored.

We do not have to dip far into the literature of modern educational dance to discover such references and the linking of "imagination" and "imaginative" with other terms which also tend to have commendatory force such as "creativity," "spontaneity" and "expression." What exactly is meant, however, is often far from clear. Indeed, there is a whole battery of such concepts (often well to the fore in discussions about dance and other arts, and likely to be somewhat indiscriminately associated with one another), which are in need of philosophical analysis, since it is impossible to formulate exact definitions which will hold for all the contexts in which the words or phrases expressing them are used. Such general terms, in fact, are precisely the sort in which philosophers are interested and which, as Peters (1966) has remarked, it would be as difficult to pin down with a neat formula as would be the concept of "love."

What then, can be meant by "fostering the imagination"? How are imaginative states of mind or activities to be characterised? In particular, what constitutes imaginative behaviour in respect of movement? How are we to judge progress (or perhaps regress) in this area? Is it possible to be imaginative without being creative or spontaneous? Does creativity entail imagination? Is imaginative activity as much a matter of intellect as of feeling? What is "movement imagination," and what role, if any, has it to play in dance?

These are typically philosophical questions, quite distinct from those of a psychological kind such as whether imaginative individuals differ from others in respect of intelligence, humour, attitudes to authority, and so on (see, for example, Hudson, 1966); and also from questions of a sociological variety such as whether particular subcultural groups differ in the kind of imagination they display, or in what they consider it to be and how they view its worth. This is not to suggest that there is no connection between these different disciplines. The concept of imagination might be modified as the result of some piece of empirical research,

1

while it is obvious that without a clear idea of *what* it is with which his investigations are concerned, which in fact means having an understanding of the concept, the researcher would be hard put to it to know what he was doing.

Such understanding is closely connected with knowing how the words "imagination," "imaginative," and so on, are used in everyday speech,* and it is by paying attention to linguistic usage that conceptual analysis is conducted. For the benefit of those unfamiliar with such a technique (and especially for those with only a nodding acquaintance who might mistakenly conclude that modern philosophy is "all about words"), it may be necessary to point out that what is involved is not a quibble about language, but an attempt to throw light on the concepts we have by looking at the ways in which we talk about them (cf. Hirst & Peters, 1970).

What has to be grasped from the start is that although for some words (especially those of the more technical sort such as "autistic," "dyslexia," "metricality," "labile," "icosahedron," or "iambic"), there is a single standardised meaning, this is not so in the case of each and every one. There is no such thing as the "real" or "essential" meaning of a great many, and we look in vain if we try to discover it. As Wittgenstein (1953), one of the chief pioneers of the twentieth century "revolution" in philosophy put it, "The meaning of a word is its use in the language." As a result of examining the various ways in which a word functions in everyday speech, and studying the special characteristics of each usage as well as taking into account their context and the intention of the speaker, we may be able to find a connection between them, or, if there is no single common feature, at least a "family resemblance"—like the members of a family, who may resemble one another without, however, sharing any one characteristic such as eye colour or gait. If, as in the case of "imagination" such a unifying feature is discernible, it is then spoken of as a "unitary" concept.

Before an attempt to establish this is begun, it is worth stressing a point already hinted at, that in general the term "imaginative" has *evaluative* as well as descriptive force; it is a term of appraisal, usually expressing approval. To see this on a school report applied to their offspring probably gladdens the hearts of most parents, and even if it does not, it is likely that it would be intended as complimentary rather than otherwise. Whatever conceptions or misconceptions prevail as to what imagination might be, it is widely regarded as a desirable attribute, and to describe someone as *un*imaginative is not usually to rate that individual highly. Furthermore, when we say to a person, "Oh, use your imagination!" we seem to be implying, rather as when we say, "Use your intelligence!" that this is something that we all have in some measure, that to fail to

* This is not to say that there is no evidence other than that of a verbal kind for having a concept, nor that the ability to employ correctly a word or phrase is a *necessary* condition for possessing the concept in question; but it is a *sufficient* condition.

use it is in some way to fall short of an expected standard, some achievement of which everyone should be capable in some degree, and which ought not to be left lying dormant, as it were.

But this tends to sound as if we are speaking of some power or inner process, some isolable mental function or faculty, with which we are all endowed and which blossoms or withers as opportunities are presented or withheld for its nourishment and exercise. This, however, is sheer nonsense. There is no *thing,* "imagination," any more than there is a substance called "gravity" or "electricity." And to suppose that it can be developed in the same sort of way as that in which the heart muscle or the biceps may be developed, is likely to lead us seriously astray in our educational thinking and practice.

It is in fact a good example of what Wittgenstein (1953) was talking about when he spoke of the "bewitchment of our intelligence by means of language." Because there is the word "imagination" it is apt to sound as if there is some entity corresponding to it, some mysterious function residing somewhere inside us, as is also likely to happen in the cases of, for example, "intelligence," "creativity," or (to take a technical concept from the field of movement), "effort." Although credit is no longer accorded to the faculty psychology fashionable in the nineteenth century (not least among educationalists, who believed, for example, that through Latin a capacity for logical thinking could be cultivated), the notion still seems to persist to some extent that through activities such as "creative writing," "creative dance," "child drama," moving freely to music, free painting and drawing, and the like, imaginative and creative powers may be directly tapped and fostered.

The idea also prevails in some quarters (and teachers of modern educational dance have been as guilty as any in claiming this) that imaginative achievements in one area can spill over into and directly improve those in others. But when it is recognised that what counts as "imagination" in, for instance, literature, is different from what constitutes "imagination" in dance, it is clear that this cannot be so. There may well be reasons, chiefly of a psychological kind (such as the motivational value of success and encouragement) why attainment in one field leads to increased efforts in another, but criteria by which imaginative performances in each case are to be judged are logically distinct.

This is brought out when we examine the various things that we have in mind when we say that, for example, a child, a teacher, a hostess, or a writer is imaginative, or apply the term "imaginatively" to the way in which a dancer, a musician, a cricketer, a military tactician or a scientist performs or acts. (It might be remarked here that we may sometimes prevent ourselves from falling victim to the "name/thing" theory of meaning, and escape the "bewitchment" by language of which Wittgenstein speaks, if we take note of the *adjectives* and *adverbs* relating to certain terms, especially mental terms, rather than concentrate on abstract nouns.)

In the above instances, it is obvious that we are likely to be singling out quite different and even contrasting qualities. We might mean by referring to a child as "imaginative" that he indulges frequently in daydreaming; or alternatively that paints vivid pictures, or invents fantastic stories, or easily identifies himself with other people or things. The same term may describe a teacher when he engages in the highly sophisticated activity of hypothesising, as for example in history or philosophy ("Let us suppose that Hitler had invaded Britain in 1940 . . ." "Take the case of a being in a world in which all sensory experiences are auditory . . ." etc.); or when, like the imaginative hostess, he shows a lively interest in those with whom he deals, and is sensitive to how they feel and respond in various situations.

In the case of a writer, "imaginative" might imply that he has a gift for describing the improbable or seemingly impossible, as with authors of science fiction, or that he has a fecundity of ideas (a certain quantitative criterion entering here, since the number of different themes that come teeming from his pen, and the rate at which they flow are contributory factors to the verdict). We might also mean that he imagines (that is, comes to *believe*), at least temporarily, that his characters and the events which he portrays are real. Similarly what is implied when we say that Paul Taylor or Yehudi Menuhin gave a most imaginative performance differs from what is referred to when we speak of Sobers' field-placing being imaginative, or of Nelson deploying his forces imaginatively at the battle of the Nile, or say, that Newton's formulating the theory of gravity as a result of seeing the apple fall from the tree was a leap of imagination. The point is that *imagining* takes many different forms. It is a many-faceted activity, not a nuclear operation common to all the instances given, as is true also of teaching, housekeeping or gardening. Like any of these it embraces a range of types of activity and is not confined, as is sometimes thought, to the field of the arts.

But this range can be grouped, and useful classifications have been made by Flew (1953) and Furlong (1961). These seem to reflect the major distinctions which philosophical discussions of the subject have between them covered over the years, though some varieties have traditionally received more consideration than others. Furlong's three categories are "in imagination," "supposing" and "with imagination." In order to distinguish and give content to the different kinds of imaginative performance that occur in connection with dance, an analysis has been worked out for the purposes of this essay which takes these distinctions into account, and it may be illustrated by taking an imaginary (!) scene in a primary school classroom and asking what kinds of things happen there that are correctly described as involving "imagination."

A teacher is about to tell a story.* She begins, "Now I want you to imagine a dark forest, with tall leafy trees . . ." And she goes on to set the scene, encouraging the children to conjure up mental pictures and sounds, and possibly images of smell, taste, touch and the kinaesthetic kind too. But from time to time she notices

---

* Neither approval nor disapproval of what this imaginary teacher does is intended!

that one of her pupils does not seem to be listening. He is staring out of the window, lost in his own thoughts. He is daydreaming, perhaps imagining himself doing other things that he would like to be doing. But, like the rest of the class, he too is engaged in imagining, only in their case this is directed from outside, i.e. by the teacher, while in his case it is *un*directed (though it could also be self-directed).

Now if it is a gloomy winter's day, with the wind moaning outside and the lights in the classroom not yet switched on, and if the teacher has built up a powerful atmosphere, it may happen that some of the children come to imagine that beyond the windows there really is a dark forest, with all the exciting and mysterious things that she is relating actually taking place. They come, that is, to believe (like the novelist in his characters) in what is not real—that is, to believe falsely. And the teacher, realising this, may have to do and say things eventually to reassure some of the nervous ones, as she has also to deal with the daydreamer (even if this is in the form of taking no action at all, which is just as positive a course as if she interrupted him). It might then be said that in coping with daydreaming, or with children who are imagining that some state of affairs obtains which in fact does not, or who are frightened, hurt, angry, disappointed, or in any other distressing state of mind, that she has to *exercise her imagination.* She has to try to project herself into their situation, to see things from their point of view, to step, as it were, into their shoes.

Finally, after the story, the teacher suggests that some children dramatise it, while others write, paint, model or do a dance in connection with it. So, in the first instance, some act, playing the part of witches, or Hansel and Gretel, and so on, i.e. they imagine themselves to be in circumstances different from the actual. Here, in saying "Imagine that you are in a dark forest . . .," she means by "imagine" something different from what she meant when she began the story. It is not conjuring up images only, or even at all, that is invited now, though this may happen as well. What is necessarily involved is physical movement and perhaps also, speech, and unlike the situation in which they were going through things "in imagination," she can now actually see or hear their imaginings, i.e. their make-believe. And from all the children, including those who are painting, dancing, writing, or modelling, the teacher probably hopes for what she calls an "imaginative" response, evidence of originality and "creative imagination."

Five major distinctions then have been drawn which will be referred to as:-

  (i)   imaging,
  (ii)  empathising,
  (iii) believing falsely (or mistakenly),
  (iv)  acting,
  (v)   using "creative imagination."

(i), *imaging,* corresponds to Furlong's "in imagination" and (v), *using "creative imagination,"* to his "with imagination," while the other three might be considered varieties of "supposing." Each will now be examined in turn, particularly in respect of their relevance to dance and to education, but it must be emphasised at the outset that these categories are neither complete nor exclusive. They have been selected solely for what seems to be their significance in a particular field. They also to some extent overlap with one another. We may imagine both in the sense of *believing mistakenly* (iii) and of *acting* (iv) with or without *mental imagery* (i). *Acting* necessarily involves *empathising* (ii); and it may be carried on with varying degrees of *"creative imagination."* It is also worth noting that false belief may be a result of acting.


## 1. Imaging

In most philosophical discussions of imagination, attention is apt to centre on the occurrence of mental imagery, which includes not only visual images, but also auditory, olfactory, gustatory, tactual and kinaesthetic; and of these, perhaps understandably, the visual sort has received the greatest amount of treatment. But, as Flew remarks, concentration on imaging of whatever kind is misleading, because as soon as we appeal to linguistic usage, we can see that this is a rather one-sided account, and that a good deal of what is legitimately described as "imagining" may not be accompanied by images of any kind. Nevertheless, though to have a mental image is not a necessary condition for imagining, it is sufficient. To visualise, to have aural images, and so on, is *par excellence* to imagine. These are the central or paradigm cases.

A further distinction which needs to be made under this heading is that between memory images and imagination images. In one sense, of course, both concern the non-real; we do not actually see, hear, etc. But memory images arise from what we have, in fact, experienced in real life. To "remember" is a verb of the achievement or "got it" variety, as Ryle (1949) has called it. Either we do remember or we do not; it is a contradiction to speak of remembering inaccurately or incorrectly—we are just not remembering at all. In principle, therefore, memory images are verifiable, whereas imagination images, which do not depend on what has already actually happened (though they must be derived from sense perception) are not. This notion of unreality, or at least non-reality, seems to be the key to the unitary nature of the concept, since in all its varieties it seems to involve freedom to envisage what is not the case, to see one "thing" as another, or in terms of, or in relation to another.

In our hypothetical classroom situation, two types of imaging were instanced, *un*directed, as in the case of the boy daydreaming (though, as already mentioned, this could be of the self-directed variety or an alternation of both), and directed from the *out*side, as when the teacher sought to get the children to conjure up images. In the first instance, *undirected* or *autonomous**[*]* imaging just seems to happen; images float up, as it were, without any act of will. There is a certain

---

[*] "Autonomous" and "controlled" are terms of McKellar (1957).

involuntariness in this type of activity inasmuch as we remain relatively passive as regards what images succeed one another, and in what order, though it is possible intentionally to settle into a relaxed state of receptivity which is often conducive to such reverie. (We may be perfectly well aware of what we are doing during daydreaming, and though we become partially cut off from reality in temporarily ceasing to pay attention to our immediate surroundings and whatever is going on around us, there is no question of us failing to distinguish reality from our imaginings, as in the case of hallucinations, false belief, and so on. We are able too to "switch off," so to speak, when required to do so.)

The second type. *directed* or *controlled* imaging (which may be guided from outside *or* self-directed) may either precede that of the undirected kind or follow it. That is, it is possible consciously to select an image by recalling a past experience or postulating a new one, and then use it as a starting point for a train of images which, once set in motion, becomes progressively unguided. As Furlong (1961) puts it, we can point our boat in a chosen direction and then let it take its course. Or, conversely, finding our boat drifting along a particular channel (to adapt the metaphor), we deliberately keep it going in this direction; that is, we seize hold of a picture, a musical phrase, or a group of words that seems to have "popped up," and then bring to bear on it a purposeful concentration which is quite different from the passivity which allows images to arise and multiply spontaneously.

Although daydreaming is normally considered not only *not* desirable in an educational situation, but positively *un*desirable, inasmuch as it breaks or prevents concentration on the matter in hand, it may, by contrast, be argued that to cultivate such a habit is perhaps essential to some individuals for certain kinds of activity, especially that of a creative nature. Many artists, for example, testify to the need to suspend purely conscious control and to allow unconscious processes to take over at least during some stages of composing. What part, then, may imaging play in dance or acting?

Leaving aside those stray, irrelevant images which drift up unexpectedly and perhaps have a distracting influence, as might happen during any activity, the performer may have visual images which tend to be associated with particular steps or gestures or postures within a particular sequence, and these may conceivably serve as an aid in learning or in remembering, or in helping the expression. This might seem most likely in the case of movement of a representational nature, when certain surroundings are visualised, or in a period dance; but it can also happen in, say, a "space harmony" sequence, or in a study based on the "effort cube," or in any dance in which shapes and patterns are of importance. Similarly, visual images may play an important part during listening to music, and this may influence the use that is made of it when it is to be used for dance composition. (Whether the result is good or bad is, of course, a further matter.)

This can work the other way round in respect of aural images. It can be useful for the performer to "hear" the rhythms of the movement in the absence of sound, particularly if he is composing his own accompaniment or giving a lead to another who will do so; or in practising a sequence which is to be accompanied and for which the music or other form of sound is known, so that while it is not being provided it can still be "heard" in "the mind's ear." (The latter, of course, in contrast to the former, are memory images.)

But perhaps the most interesting question from the point of view of the movement specialist is that of kinaesthetic imagery, and the part that this may play before we perform a known sequence, or as we watch other performers, or moving objects, or listen to music, or simply lie in bed (when it is the experience of many dancers and others to continue to "feel" in the muscles the movements which have been rehearsed during the day). This again is a case of the muscles "remembering," but it is also possible to imagine muscular sensations that we have never actually had, i.e. imagination images. If we can read music we can look at a score and "hear" the tune in our head, as also we can auralise the rhythms and cadences of printed words, even though we have never heard them before in that particular order, nor even occasionally, some of the words. Similarly, by studying movement notation we may get the feel of a dance sequence previously unknown to us.

In this connection it is interesting to note a passage in Laban's "Principles of Dance and Movement Notation":-

> A skilled reader of movement notation can not only understand what the body of the dancer does, but he can shudder or smile on deciphering the mental and emotional contents of the symbols . . . a dancer can see with his inner eye the movements of the human body while reading the dance notation.

Here there is no mention of *kinaesthetic* imagery, as might perhaps have been expected; this is the point of view of the observer rather than of the performer. It is indeed understandable that *visualising* both group shape and group movement, as well as of an individual body, might be very typical of how some choreographers and producers work.

Whether or not they tend to be strong visualisers, just as many musical composers apparently have strong aural images (Mozart, for example, is said to have heard whole symphonies in imagination before writing them down), and whether perhaps dancers have a well-developed capacity for kinaesthetic imagery, what is important to note in all these cases of imaging is that *they are not in themselves observable occurrences.* Whatever can or cannot be discovered about a person as a result of observing his physical behaviour, this is *not* something that can be so ascertained. The only evidence there can be is the individua''s own testimony, and he can therefore be described as "imaginative" in this sense only on his own account.

What follows logically from this fact that mental images are essentially private experiences, which is of the greatest significance for educators, is that if they are to be communicated to others this can be achieved *only through the use of public symbols.* Flew (1953) is apt to speak as if their description is restricted to verbal communication, but this is patently not so, and moreover many images are not capable of literal translation at all. This of course by no means renders them in any way inferior to those which do appropriately find expression in words, but the symbols which embody them are of a wholly different order from linguistic symbols. If it were otherwise, all painting, sculpture, music and dance compositions, for example, would lose their particular significance.

When, as educators, we speak of developing the imagination, it is therefore clear that we must be talking primarily of developing the ability to understand and use symbols. It involves the initiation of children into a variety of public "languages," each with its own distinctive techniques, procedures and disciplines, whether the material be words, paint, clay, sound or movement. Even if we knew how to induce particular mental images we could hardly, as educators, set out *simply* to do this. Unless they are helped to translate them into public terms, it is difficult to see what educational purpose such a procedure could serve.

## 2. Empathising

Imaginative or unimaginative behaviour in relation to other people is often described also as "sensitive" or "insensitive." What does this mean? As with imaging, has it perhaps something to do with envisaging what is not actually the case? That is, although we are not, and never can be in the *same* situation as another person, we can come near to putting ourselves into his position. While it is impossible to think another's thoughts, have his feelings or experience his sensations (if this were so, they would no longer be that individual's, but our own), we can nevertheless pause to consider what it might be like to be, as we say, in someone else's shoes; we can to some extent step outside ourselves and try to identify with him. A teacher, a hostess or a counsellor who is spoken of as "imaginative" is one who is recognised as doing just this, whether at a conscious level or more intuitively.

A necessary step in responding to someone in an understanding and sympathetic way is to appreciate in some measure how that person appraises and therefore feels about a situation; sympathy, in the sense of exercising practical care and concern for others, presupposes empathy. This is an important aspect of moral development and moral education, about both of which comparatively little is known, but to which dance, as well as other forms of physical education, may have a significant, though incidental, contribution to make. Such a claim depends on the fact, firstly, that many of the judgments we make about a person's state of mind are based on the inferences we draw from his physical behaviour—and this, of course, not simply in terms of *what* he says and does, but from *how* he speaks and moves; and secondly, that putting oneself into another's position, either by impersonating or trying to assess the situation from his point of view, is part of what is necessarily involved in certain curriculum activities.

To take the second point first. In imitating someone, that is, reproducing not merely a few movement clichés in the way that we might adopt a few of his favourite sayings or copy items of his dress, but the rhythms and spatial patterns as well as bodily details of his movement (including "shadow movements"),* we do seem to gain some special insight into what it is to *be* that person; it seems to be more than a superficial, external set of particulars that we assume. And in situations of unrehearsed group interplay, such as giving or following a lead, "shadowing," "mirroring," or in other ways adapting and responding to the movement of others, it is obviously essential to observe how they move and how they respond to our movement, and to consider what "openings" are provided them (or denied) by what we do. In other words, we are required to *imagine* what it is like for them to be in a particular situation, and we *learn* what kinds of interaction are possible and appropriate in specific situations. It is just not possible, for example, for the leader of a wedge-shaped group to make sudden and sharp changes of direction and yet to keep the formation of the group intact; nor can a member of a file, picking up a wave-like flow of movement passed on sequentially along the line, go into action at the right moment, "entering on cue," as it were, unless he attends closely to the timing (and possibly also the shape)of the movement of the whole group, and especially, of course, of those on each side of him.

"Taking the attitude of the other," to use a phrase of Mead (1934), is also required in many games, from those such as chess to the fast-moving team variety, since there has to be constant anticipation of the moves of others, whether they be opponents or collaborators. It characterises too activities ranging from that of the politician engaged in debate to that of the military tactician; trying to foresee the moves of others, in order either to block or outmanoeuvre them demands the seeing of things from their point of view, and taking up positions not the individual's own. (Hence the non-real aspect of this brand of imaginative activity.) To say that George Best plays imaginative football, therefore, or that Kennedy's action at the time of the Cuban crisis was an act of imaginative statesmanship, is a perfectly legitimate way of using the term.

However, since in most of these cases the intention is to outwit, defeat or at least score off one's opponent(s), and to further one's own cause, their value as a means of furthering sympathetic insight into other people's feelings and responses is doubtful. By contrast this *is* what is involved in drama and in some kinds of dance (i.e. when it deals with human problems and passions as distinct from exclusively kinetic ideas). The close observation and understanding of the significance of bodily movement and position required by participating either as a performer or a spectator are related to the appreciation of gesture and posture as expressive of feeling, even though this expression is *symbolic* in an art form and not *symptomatic* (cf. Langer, 1953).

There is, of course, no reason to assume that such experience will automatically

* See p. 36 below.

lead to imaginative and sensitive behaviour in relation to other people in real-life situations. Indeed the cynic might say that those who engage in dancing and acting are apt to be less, rather than more, sensitive to the feelings of others, being so often immersed in their own or concerned with their display! If, however, this were indeed the case, it would argue not for an abandoning of dance and drama as educational activities, but for more rigorous initiation into them as forms of aesthetic understanding, in order that the notion be dispelled that they are to be pursued because of the opportunities they offer for cathartic release and self-expression of the undisciplined, outpouring kind.

Nevertheless, although relationships within dance and drama are not *personal* (see Essay C, section 3, below), it does not seem unreasonable to suppose that such activities *can* illuminate and influence actual everyday experience inasmuch as knowledge of human behaviour is integral to them. In this connection it is difficult to see why a movement education conceived of in broader, yet more precise terms than at present should not include a study of such behaviour in real-life situations, as distinct from within the context of dance and drama. Many people's observations of the expressive features of movement are confined to rather crude generalisations in terms of *items* of behaviour, such as tapping one's foot, fiddling with one's clothing, rubbing one's nose, etc., rather than the more subtle aspects of rhythmic phrasing and spatial change. Yet many are aware, in a vague, half-conscious way, of "messages" and "cues" which are given, even though unintentionally, by others, and much might be done to strengthen and refine this tendency (see Essay C, section 3, below).

Clearly, however, the interpretation of such observations in terms of mood, feeling, emotion, and so on, is *learned,* and both this and the noting of particular kinds of details which may be picked out require guidance from those who have the appropriate knowledge and skills. These things do not just happen, nor should they be left to chance. Consistent and systematic training is needed to ensure accurate and objective analysis of movement and to prevent facile and stereotyped judgments of what is seen.

### 3. Believing falsely

It is well known that George IV imagined during all his later life that he had been at the battle of Waterloo. Similarly a person may imagine that he is Julius Caesar, or that he is covered with spots or suffering from some incurable disease when in fact he is not. It goes without saying that imagining in this sense, i.e. of believing falsely, has nothing to do with education. Indeed it is not an activity at all, but a state of mind, and in its extreme form is a pathological condition, something that the victim of the delusion cannot help.

Nevertheless, something akin to it, more particularly in its temporary and less serious form, such as in the example of the children who came to suppose mistakenly that there *was* a dark forest outside, is of some interest and importance in connection with education, since it raises the question of how far anyone impersonating another comes to believe, even though only temporarily, that he really is someone else. With children it is often the case that they take the imaginary for the real *as a result* of acting; make-believe passes into belief. They forget, so it seems, that it all began with "Let's pretend."* Actors, on the other hand, usually deliberately try to "get inside the part" beforehand, and it might be thought that they would give their most convincing performance when they are, as it were, "lost" in the role. Some indeed claim that they do "become," on each occasion, e.g. Othello, or Jocasta, forgetting who in fact they are, that they are playing before an audience, and so on.

But if this is so, it follows that they are no longer imagining in the sense of acting, but are in the grip of an illusion and cut off from reality. The result is not art but mental disorder. There is a famous case of an opera singer, Anna Moffo, who during her rendering of a scene in which the character she was enacting had a heart attack, herself apparently had all the symptoms of such a malady and had to be carried off the stage (quoted in Lawrie, 1967). She had identified so strongly with the part that she had, in effect, become absorbed into it and lost touch with her real self.

Even if imagining of this type were effective, however (and assuming that methods could be found of encouraging it to happen), it could hardly be justified as educational, since to put individuals in situations in which they become unaware of what is happening to them is to fail to treat them as autonomous agents capable of rational choice and reflective self-direction. The whole idea of children being "taken out of themselves" is, indeed, one which demands rigorous re-examination on the part of educators; being absorbed *into* something has to be distinguished from being absorbed or involved *with* it. (See pp. 96-97 below.)

## 4. Acting

The fact that such a case as that of the opera singer quoted in the previous section is rare argues that, far from failing to distinguish what is imagined from what is actual, the successful actor or dancer is highly conscious of what he is doing and must, in some measure, be "distanced" from it (cf. Bullough, 1912). As Ryle (1949) mentions in his discussion of imagination, a person engaged in pretending has to be alert, "non-absent-minded," and apply his mind to the part he plays. Moreover, as he also points out, pretending involves not only *having* but also *using* knowledge. We cannot, that is, play a part without knowing something of what it is to be, or do, that which we imitate; and when we pretend we are utilising knowledge we already possess. It is knowledge in action.

---

* This is not to equate pretending with acting, but the differences are of no consequence for the purposes of this discussion.

The fact that acting may be regarded thus, i.e. as a manifestation or even a test of knowledge, has certain important consequences for education. It has to be granted that if someone can play a part, he *knows* how another individual, or type of individual, behaves, or would behave, under certain circumstances, even though he may be unable to give a verbal description. In Ryle's words:-

> The business of trying to behave in ways in which a cross man would behave is itself, in part, the thought of how he would behave . . . . Mimicking him *is* thinking how he behaves.

Thus the imaginings of young or inarticulate children, which do not always readily find expression in words (even though they are capable of verbal translation), are often manifest in movement. Furthermore, the act of giving public utterance to their ideas and attitudes through non-verbal means may not only crystallise and reinforce what *they* know, but also provide insight for those who watch, both into the apparently familiar, and into the individual himself and the way in which he apprehends (which includes feeling as well as thinking about) the world.

This is not, of course, to suggest either that dramatic and dance activities are educationally valuable only for the young and inarticulate (though they might be considered to have some special place for them in the curriculum); nor that their language development can be left to take care of itself on the assumption that this is not so important provided that they can symbolise their experience somehow. In any case, in the field of dance acting is often not involved at all. It does, however, sometimes happen that, as a result of movement training presented solely in terms of bodily, rhythmic and spatial details, imagining of this kind occurs because of the associations of the 'feel' or appearance of the movement. Travelling swiftly and lightly over the ground and stopping abruptly every now and then, for instance, often sets up responses among Junior school children of pretending to be burglars or Red Indians, pausing on the balls of the feet then running and simultaneously dropping low only to rise up again, responses of 'being' aeroplanes, birds and the like. Even though such was not the original intention, it is clearly important for the teacher to be aware that happenings of this kind are likely to ensue, to decide what exactly the purpose of such experience is, and to take steps accordingly.

## 5. Using "creative imagination"

Furlong (1961), taking Ryle's example of the child playing bears, says of his own description of this as "with imagination":-

> By this I mean, roughly, that his play shows originality, creativeness, . . . His play is, in its own way, a minor work of art, a product of intelligence and sympathy. It is a work of imagination . . . . He is not merely reproducing, merely imitating: there is an original streak in his performance.

And it is probably in this sense that most teachers in the field of movement are likely to speak of "imagination." But, as indicated at the beginning of this essay, "originality," "spontaneity," "creativity," and the like are somewhat vague terms. As Hudson (1966) remarks of the last:-

> This odd word . . . covers everything from answers to a particular psychological test, to forming a good relationship with one's wife . . . (It) applies to all those qualities of which psychologists approve.

(And we might add, along with psychologists, educationists!)

For many teachers, "creative" activities still seem to refer to those of a special kind in which children for example, paint, model, write and dance *freely,* i.e. in conditions of a permissive sort where specific direction is lacking as to what is to be done with the materials available, whether colours, clay, movement or sound. They are expected to give free rein to their own ideas and feelings with the minimum of interference from the teacher. Any suggestion of him instructing, demonstrating, or passing on his ideas and knowledge ("imposing" as it is somewhat emotively called), is deplored; and imitation on the part of the children, learning by watching him, or mastering a specific technique is regarded as leading not only to failure to develop creativity and imagination but to its actual thwarting and stunting. (Here we see the influence of the old faculty psychology still at work.)

Bound up with such procedures are aims which are not specifically educational at all, such as the playing out of fantasies, the discharging of emotional tensions, and the experiencing of exuberant release, or at least, deeply satisfying pleasure. Though these might well be *by-products* of genuine educational activities, as *aims* they belong to the sphere of psychotherapy. Dance and drama are particularly liable to suffer from these mistaken views because of the close connection between feeling and its bodily expression. Even among those who reject what has been called "the corked bottle theory of the emotions," and the suggestion that art activities serve to remove this "cork," so-called creative dance tends to imply using the body in an uninhibited, unconventional manner. Thus it is often associated with spontaneity and originality. Russell (1958), for example, discussing the need for teachers to provide some sort of stimulus for invention and composition says:-

> . . . often natural spontaneity and a lively movement imagination have been lost through lack of fostering in the very young . . .

And Ullmann (1960) speaks of "satisfaction of one's play sense, using imagination and spontaneous action" alongside reference to "exercise of one's formative drive, combining creative faculty with reflective powers."

It is not immediately obvious why spontaneity should be looked upon as an unquestionably desirable quality in itself, nor how it could be promoted in a general way as a result of participating in "creative" or "expressive" activities. But it is clear that if it is held that for dance to be educational it must be of this character (a claim requiring justification),* then it will be advantageous to exploit the apparent readiness of young children to indulge in dance-like activity without much thought or prompting. It will be seen as desirable, before they become hampered by preconceived notions of stylised dance, to seek to preserve this tendency to allow unplanned, unformulated movement to bubble up and overflow, as it were, rather in the way in which adults from time to time break out into humming or little snatches of song.

The sporadic outbursts of impulsive, rhythmic movement that is delighted in by any healthy young creature, be it lamb, foal, puppy, kitten or child (such as, for example, Douglas Kennedy describes so well) are not, however, well-described as "creative" or "imaginative." Such movements are often accidental, unintentional and incapable of being repeated; they are rarely consciously selected or organised in relation to one another, and it seems odd to speak of creating something when it happens in such an unconsidered and haphazard manner.

It may well be, of course, that a spontaneous response to a stimulus such as music or a poem, or what is called "movement play" has a valuable part in the early stages of a dance composition (though it is by no means either a necessary stage or the only way to start); but it is misleading to call such activity "original" or "imaginative," unless by these terms we simply mean the doing of something which the individual has never done before. It would indeed be surprising if this did not happen with children growing and developing normally. Moreover, on this account, a movement which is imitated, but which is performed for the first time would be original, and this is the very antithesis of what is usually implied when children are spoken of as "creative" or "responding imaginatively."

As White (1968) has pointed out, when we refer to originality in the case of an adult we mean that he is breaking away from the orthodox and the conventional. Originality has written into it the intention to produce something different, and this in turn implies a knowledge of what the conventional standards are, what it is against which he is reacting. But this is not what a child is doing when he spontaneously capers and twirls about. However unusual in the adult's eyes a child's prancings may seem (and often, in fact, they are quite stereotyped, conforming very largely to the sort of thing that many children do at a particular stage), they can hardly be counted as original or imaginative if they occur without reference to existing practices, and without the understanding and deliberate intent which make a "differing from" possible.

There is too the further point which White raises in connection with art activities, as to how far originality is a criterion of aesthetic value anyway. Certainly it is not sufficient. As Dilman (1967) makes clear, those whose imaginative achievements, whether in art or science, transform our vision and

---

*See Essay C, section 2a.

deepen our understanding are often most heavily indebted to an established line of thought or way of doing things, and steeped in the inherited ideas and techniques of a particular discipline, yet are able at once to follow a tradition and depart from set practices. But just because someone breaks out of a tradition and succeeds in being different it does not follow that his work is of any merit; it may be merely odd, contrived, straining for effect.

Nor is originality a necessary condition. Many works of art, from sonnets to symphonies, do not involve radical innovation, but conform to a standardised pattern or prototype. At a somewhat more modest level, there are also activities of the kind in which one works within a given framework (e.g. a piece of "motif writing")* and which do not require originality of the highest order, but which nevertheless lead to the production of an aesthetic object.† Similarly, for children who are capable of distinguishing, for example, motifs, repetitions, contrasts, developments, and so on, to learn a set dance-study and then to be helped to produce variations on or additions to it, is not only a useful step towards creativity "proper," as has sometimes been suggested, but is, in itself, creative and imaginative activity.

This brings out the same feature which has been seen to characterise other types of imagining so far considered, that of seeing things in a way different from how they actually or already are. Indeed this is what distinguishes the achievements of people to whom "creative" and "imaginative" are extended *specifically on account of those achievements.* What is of importance here is that these terms are not applied in respect of private mental experience such as having images, nor some special kind of thought-process, nor of doing as one likes in conditions thought to be conducive to the release of a unique sort of inner energy (perhaps in a therapeutic rather than a strictly educative way), such as having a range of materials for unguided exploration. They refer instead to public artefacts and performances judged to be of excellence according to the standards characteristic of the particular activity or discipline in question.

Thus not only artists, but also scientists, philosophers, chefs, fashion-designers, producers, and a host of others operate *with imagination* in the combining and arranging (or recombining and re-arranging) of elements previously unconnected or in a different relationship. Just as we can create a mental image of something not known in the world of sense, such as pink snow, consisting nevertheless of elements which are derived from perceptual experience (i.e. pinkness and snow), so in dance composition, for example, the rhythms and spatial components of movement are consciously organised and synthesised into a new complexity. But whereas our image of pink snow is essentially a private experience, the dance is available for

---

*A shorthand version of Kinetography Laban (see Preston-Dunlop, 1969).

† This term is used in this context in preference to "work of art" (which is apt to suggest a masterpiece, or at least a sophisticated artefact), in order to embrace the achievements of children which may yet have some measure of aesthetic merit.

public appraisal and evaluation. To become capable of using "creative imagination" in the making of dance requires, therefore, as in any other field of activity in which imaginative achievements are sought, skilled and informed teaching by someone who has knowledge of dance composition; mere faith in some mysterious faculty is not enough.

What then of "movement imagination" (Laban 1950, 1960)? Is not this something unique to invention and composition in respect of movement? Clearly it cannot be thought to describe some special kind of mental process, but would appear to refer to what is involved in dealing exclusively with kinetic ideas as distinct from using movement as a symbol of emotional feeling or literal ideas. Just as the musician has to learn to think in terms of sound and cultivate a sensitive "ear," and the painter to think in terms of colour, texture, shape, and so on, thus gaining a discriminating "eye" for such things, so the dancer's "movement" sense must be sharpened in respect of the rhythmic and spatial structures of movement and the aesthetic significance of their relation to one another. While inspiration for dance may come from a variety of sources, the stimulus peculiar to the dancer is that arising from his response to kinaesthetic sensations, though obviously this in itself is not sufficient in order to learn to compose and appreciate movement as an art form.

In addition to considering what it is to be "imaginative" from the point of view of *creating* aesthetic objects, we must now examine this idea in relation to *performance*. Here again, it is being maintained that just as the criteria which determine what is an imaginative composition are the same as those which obtain in assessing its aesthetic value, so an imaginative rendering of a dance, a song, etc., is one which reaches standards of excellence belonging to that particular activity. In saying that someone's interpretation of say, Petroushka, was most imaginative, we do not mean something over and above what constitutes a first-rate performance; it is a way of referring to the measure of its worth, not to excellence of a different kind. *[Imagination and Performance]*

This is not to suggest of course that all that is demanded is a high level of skill and craftsmanship as regards details of technical execution, though these certainly are essential. What is also entailed is the performer's understanding of and insight into the composition, and these become manifest in the performance; the dancing, the playing, the singing, *is* the understanding. A knowledge of what goes to make a created form is therefore indispensable; this is a logical truth, not one requiring empirical demonstration. It does not, however, follow from this that such knowledge must be acquired by practical experience of composing, though it seems reasonable to suppose that understanding *might* be deepened by this means.

On the whole, there is a tendency in the field of education to make the unwarranted assumption that this *is* in fact the best way, even to proceed perhaps as if it were the only way. In modern educational dance what is performed is often what has been composed by the performer, or group of performers. But obviously this need not be so. To dance imaginatively (as also to dance "expressively"), does not require that the individual concerned has himself invented the movement, any more than is the case when he acts a part in a play which he has not written, reads another's poem, or sings or plays a musical composition not his own. (And any claim that he is a better interpretative artist for being also a creative one would have to be validated by empirical inquiry.)

It may be too that there is a reluctance among some teachers to introduce specific techniques to children in the belief that this may inhibit imagination and stifle the creative impulse. While it is essential that a dance programme does not consist *simply* of training sessions, nor involve learning only *one* style or set of skills such as belong to, for example, classical ballet, or Graham technique, it is none the less of the highest importance that progressive and systematic mastery of movement is achieved. Children do not just *become* able to balance in a variety of positions, leap high in the air, execute turns, falls, and so on, with increasing control and in a diversity of ways, any more than they "come upon" ways of selecting and organising such possibilities into a coherent whole, or "stumble across" the understanding of what makes a dance. Failure to provide the means to develop an increasing range of skill in respect of bodily, rhythmic and spatial aspects of movement, whether through demonstration, explanation, experiment, or learning by discovery, etc. is, far from encouraging imaginative performance, likely to lead at best to repetition and mediocrity, at worst to sloppiness, crudity and sentimentality.

**Imagination and Appreciation**    Finally, in the realm of art there is the possibility of *imaginative looking and listening*. Although the question of originality does not arise here, it may not be stretching the concept too far to regard aesthetic appreciation as constituting an exercise of imagination. Many writers insist that it involves an act of *creative* imagination. Hospers (1946), for example, holds that:-

> In great poetry we at once receive and create an imaginative vision of the world; a new world becomes acutely presented to us, or, as Coleridge says, the poet makes us creators after him, of such a new world.

And Dewey, who long ago drew attention to the intensely active nature of aesthetic contemplation when he (1934) wrote:-

> It involves surrender. But adequate yielding of the self is possible only through a controlled activity that may well be intense . . . . Perception is an act of the going-out of energy in order to receive, not a withholding of energy . . .

compares the activity of the viewer or listener with that of the artist himself, and underlines its *synthesising* character:-

> For to perceive, a beholder must *create* his own experience . . . . Without an act of re-creation the object is not perceived as a work of art. The artist selected, simplified, clarified, abridged and condensed according to his interest. The beholder must go through these operations according to his point of view and interest . . . . In both, there is . . . a gathering together of details and particulars physically scattered into an experienced whole.

In aesthetic appreciation a special kind of effort is therefore necessary. A particular sort of attention and concentration is brought to bear on the object, so that relationships are abstracted and unobvious likenesses and contrasts detected. In dance, for example, such things as motifs, themes, variations, inversions and recapitulations may be recognised. To put it negatively, exercising imagination in this, as in other respects, implies not being restricted to perceiving in one way. As Ishiguro (1966) describes it, it is:-

> the skill . . . which enables one to be susceptible to seeing various aspects, or stop oneself from being captured by one aspect one sees . . .

And this, she adds, "seems as important as training oneself to reason."

Thus, in aesthetic education children have to be helped to see and hear what might otherwise be easily missed—for example, the relationship and significance within the total structure of a dance of such things as flux and stillness, of the held position and the gesture which leads into or follows it, and of one phrase, one rhythm and another; and the interplay of dynamic stress and varying time intervals, of sharpness and smoothness, of roundedness and angularity, of delicacy and forcefulness, and so on. These things are not just *there*. like facts of nature lying all around us, waiting to be experienced and discovered. They are not perceived in the way that cold or light or stickiness, for instance, are perceived, any more than is a cube, a stamen, or musical counterpoint. And just as these require someone who does recognise such things to point them out and explain them to us, or put us on the road to finding out that there is literally more than meets the eye in these cases, so also do even the simplest elements and constructions in movement. In Oakeshott's (1967) telling words:-

> To initiate a pupil into the world of human achievement is to make available to him much that does not lie upon the surface of his present world.

Certainly a good deal that there is to understand and appreciate in dance is not written on its face, so to speak, and to make it available to others is part of what is involved in developing imagination in this area.

This facet of dance education tends to be somewhat underestimated in schools today. There are no doubt many good reasons why there is concentration on the creating and performing aspects of dance—some of a practical nature such as the relative lack of good artefacts, as compared with our easy access to literature, music, paintings, drama, etc.; some technical such as the difficulties of arranging for live performances (though to some extent films can meet a need here); some historical, dance in schools in this country being largely regarded as a branch of physical education, or at best part of the physical education programme, and thus as involving physical movement; and, by no means least, the influence of Rudolf Laban's ideas of "educational" dance as essentially a participatory rather than a spectatorial activity.

But there is too perhaps a failure to recognise that a child's concept of what a dance *is* is likely to be unduly impoverished if there are few opportunities to see and appraise the more accomplished works of others. One has only to consider how poverty-stricken our notions of music and poetry would be if these had been limited to what we ourselves had invented; and to recall the marked improvement and desire to improve that often attend children's own efforts following the extension of their experience in this way. Conversely, creating and performing dances would seem likely to contribute to imaginative looking. Thus the practical and appreciation aspects are mutually enriching.


## Conclusion

To be "imaginative" in the aesthetic realm, therefore, demands knowledge and understanding of the standards and techniques peculiar to the art form in question. For a teacher simply to tell children to use their imagination and expect something of value to flow forth without doing anything to help them to structure their ideas, and to ensure that they have something worth expressing in the first place, is indefensible in education. Indeed it is probably erroneous to think in terms of there being determinate thoughts and feelings which first exist and then "get expressed." Rather, they come into existence, and become known, in the very formulating of the symbols involved (cf. Wollheim, 1971). Expressed differently they would *be* different. Oakeshott (1962) writes:-

> As I understand it, a poetic utterance (a work of art) is not the 'expression' of an experience, it *is* the experience and the only one there is. A poet does not do *three* things: first experience or observe or recollect an emotion, then contemplate it, and finally seek a means of expressing the results of his contemplation; he does *one* thing only, he imagines poetically.

As educators, we are not engaged in a therapeutic task, but are committed to initiating children and students into "the world of human achievement" (Oakeshott, 1967) which is constituted by a variety of public modes of experience (see also Hirst & Peters, 1970). As far as dance is concerned, this means that they engage in an *aesthetic* form of understanding, that they learn both to "speak" and to "listen" to this "voice" which contributes to the "conversation" of mankind (cf. Oakeshott, 1962). A confused, private "babbling" will not do.

To what extent every individual should compose his own dances, perform those of others, and be a spectator is, of course, a further question which depends on a great variety of considerations, and is obviously beyond the scope of this essay. Similarly, matters concerning the selection of content and methods appropriate to various age-groups and types of ability fall outside the range of conceptual inquiry.

What is clear, however, is that we cannot just say that the aim of such an enterprise is to "develop the imagination." This, as we have seen, has no meaning until it is spelled out in terms of a particular kind of activity. Although, as was pointed out earlier, there may be, and often is, an interlocking and overlapping of *imaging,* various kinds of *supposing,* and *using "creative imagination,"* imaginative behaviour in one sense is no guarantee of an imaginative performance in another. Nor is imaginative achievement of the creative kind to be expected to lead automatically to similarly-styled achievements in a different area. The imaginative physicist may or may not be also an imaginative actor or writer; but if he is, it will be because he has studied and practised the specific disciplines of that activity, and not because in some mysterious way his abilities in the scientific sphere in respect of "imaginative thinking" are immediately transferable to another realm.

The most that can be said in this connection is that such an individual might be likely to adopt a similar sort of *approach* to other undertakings upon which he embarks. His manner of *tackling* them might have a generally "imaginative" flavour in the sense of a readiness "to be susceptible to seeing various aspects" and to stop himself "from being captured by one aspect . . ." But in order for the *outcome* to be of a high quality he must necessarily apply himself to the principles and techniques of the activity in question.

As far as dance education is concerned, the implications are obvious. As McKellar (1957) has emphasised:-

Selection, reasoning, craftsmanship and hard thinking all play an essential part in artistic thought products. So also does *learning*. Before an artist can produce an acceptable work of art he must learn a great deal from others.

In so-called "creative" dance it is vital that teachers become able to evaluate their pupils' progress not simply in psychological terms such as increased confidence, better powers of concentration and involvement, a capacity to enjoy what they are doing, and such like (none of which is denied may be of considerable importance in relation to the ultimate aim), but according to criteria which apply in respect of imaginative achievements in the art form of dance. *

## References

BULLOUGH E. (1912) 'Psychical distance' as a factor in art and an aesthetic principle. Republished (1960) in M. Rader (Ed.) "A Modern Book of Aesthetics". (3rd. edit.) New York: Holt, Rinehart & Winston.

DEWEY J. (1934) "Art as Experience". New York: Capricorn.

DILMAN I. (1967) Imagination. *Proc. Arist. Soc. Supp.* Vol. **XLI**, 19-36.

FLEW A. (1953) Images, supposing and imagining. *Philosophy,* **XXVIII**, 246-254.

FURLONG E.J. (1961) "Imagination". London: Allen & Unwin.

HIRST P.H. & PETERS R.S. (1970) "The Logic of Education". London: Routledge & Kegan Paul.

HOSPERS J. (1946) "Meaning and Truth in the Arts". Chapel Hill: Univ. of N. Carolina Press.

HUDSON L. (1966) "Contrary Imaginations". London: Methuen.

ISHIGURO H. (1966) Imagination. In A. Montefiore & B. Williams (Eds.) "British Analytical Philosophy". London: Routledge & Kegan Paul.

LABAN R. (1950) "Mastery of Movement on the Stage". London: Macdonald & Evans.

LABAN R. (1956) "Principles of Dance and Movement Notation". London: Macdonald & Evans.

LABAN R. (1960) "Mastery of Movement" (2nd. edit. revised L. Ullmann). London: Macdonald & Evans.

LANGER S.K. (1953) "Feeling and Form". London: Routledge & Kegan Paul.

LAWRIE J.M.S. (1967) Persons and personality. Unpublished doctoral dissertation, London University.

MCKELLAR P. (1957) "Imagination and Thinking: a psychological analysis". London: Cohen & West.

MEAD G.H. (1934) "Mind, Self and Society". Chicago: Univ. Press.

OAKESHOTT M. (1962) The voice of poetry in the conversation of mankind. In "Rationalism in Politics and other Essays". London: Methuen.

OAKESHOTT M. (1967) Learning and teaching. In R.S. Peters (Ed.) "The Concept of Education". London: Routledge & Kegan Paul.

PETERS R.S. (1966) "Ethics and Education". London: Allen & Unwin.

PRESTON-DUNLOP V. (1969) "Practical Kinetography Laban". London: Macdonald & Evans.

RUSSELL J. (1958) "Modern Dance in Education". London: Macdonald & Evans.

RYLE G. (1949) "The Concept of Mind". London: Hutchinson.

ULLMANN L. (1960) Movement education. *L.A.M.G.Mag.,* **24**, 19-28.

WHITE J.P. (1968) Creativity and education: a philosophical analysis. *B.J.E.S.,* **XVI**, 2, 123-137.

WITTGENSTEIN L. (1953) "Philosophical Investigations". Oxford: Blackwell.

WOLLHEIM R. (1971) Talking about aesthetics. *The Listener,* **85, 2186,** 201-204.

# B

# EFFORT

# B EFFORT
## PART 1

A key concept in the study and practice of movement as initiated by Rudolf Laban is that of "effort."

As far as can be established neither this term, nor any German equivalent, was used by Laban prior to his coming to England in 1938, though the idea is closely related to, and sometimes seems identical with that of "eukinetics," that aspect of movement which deals with the study of its dynamic and rhythmic content, as distinct from (though essentially interrelated with) its spatial structure. In a footnote referring to "eukinetics" in the posthumously published book "Choreutics" (1966), Lisa Ullmann, who was responsible for annotating and editing the manuscript (written in 1940), states:-

> Laban introduced this term many years ago when he explored the laws of harmony within kinetic energy. Later he expanded this field of study and called it "effort" . . .

This mention of "eukinetics" occurs in the context of a discussion which includes reference to ballet terminology. Such terms as "battu," "glissé," "fouetté," etc. indicate, Laban claims, a long-standing recognition not only of the elements of force and time and their varying combinations in space, but also of the importance of these in the observation of movement generally, and in dance teaching in particular. But impetus to the later development of his "eukinetic" theories came not from his work in the theatre (as in the case of his "space harmony" ideas), but from his experience in industry and education, and *Effort* (1947), his first book to be published in England, and in English, was the direct result of his war-time collaboration with F.C. Lawrence, an industrialist and management consultant, who is also the co-author.

Far from being introduced as a specialised, technical term, however, "effort" is used throughout the Preface in its most general sense, extending to work, human relationships, art and education. Often it could be replaced by "exertion(s)" or "activity"/"activities." As a preliminary to investigating the various uses which it comes to have in Laban's writings, it would therefore seem profitable to examine the way the word functions in ordinary language. As pointed out in the previous essay, this is not to engage in a verbal quibble. Laban could have used "effort" in any special way he chose, or, as he frequently did to considerable advantage in the absence of adequate terms, coined a new one (as in the case of "kinesphere" and "choreutics," for example). There is nothing to prevent anyone from making a stipulative definition of an existing word, provided that he gives notice of how he intends to use that term, and then consistently adheres to this. Since Laban is reputed to have selected "effort" with some care, however, we are entitled to expect that it will carry at least some of its usual connotations unless and until we are informed differently. While this does happen to some extent in *Modern Educational Dance* (1948) and *Mastery of Movement on the Stage* (1950), no clear indication of any departure from standard usage is given in *Effort* (1947).

Three interrelated notions of some importance for this inquiry emerge from an "appeal to language." First, it implies activity rather than passivity; secondly, it is bound up with intentions and aims; and thirdly, it denotes striving of some kind, often against difficulties or obstacles. To elaborate:-
1.    It refers to human beings *doing* something, not to things *happening* to them. We *make* an effort (or efforts); we exert ourselves, we are not in the grip of some force. However, it is not confined to human activity. We speak of animals making efforts to escape, to protect their young, and so on. But we do *not* (and this is of some significance in view of the way in which Laban sometimes talks), attribute it to inanimate phenomena, except perhaps in speaking graphically, as when we describe the tides as beating against the cliffs in an effort to engulf the land, or the wind as attempting to tug the washing off the line. Though we commonly refer to the sun trying to break through the clouds, we do so knowing that we are speaking figuratively. Only a child or an extremely unsophisticated person would believe otherwise. Perhaps however in the case of plants a certain ambiguity does arise, because it may sound correct to describe a shoot as making an effort to pierce the soil or reach towards the light. But it is clear that plants have no choice. This is not *behaviour,* much less is it *conduct;* it is merely response to stimuli. This brings us to the second point, that of intention.
2.·   Efforts are directly related to goals and purposes, they meet with success or failure. Hence we may say that our efforts were rewarded or that they were all in vain. If a teacher lamenting to a colleague that he has been wasting his efforts with 4G, replies to the question "Why? What were you hoping to achieve?" with "Oh, nothing in particular—but my efforts were wasted all the same," we should find this nonsense. The whole idea of effort is unintelligible without that of an aim or end.
3.    Finally, in the pursuit of a goal, making an effort suggests encountering some kind of obstacle or resistance, either internal or external. Thus when we say "It was an effort to get up this morning," we refer to having to overcome an inclination to stay in bed. A child described as making an effort to play would be assumed to be finding difficulty, say, because he was unwell or feeling miserable or, alternatively,

because he did not know what to do, as in the case of a game where certain procedures and rules must be understood. The fact that we do not employ the term in situations where what we do comes easily is borne out by our use of the antonym "effortless," which generally applies to unstrained or unhampered performance.

In this connection it is interesting to note two distinct meanings given in the Oxford English Dictionary:-

(i)     "abstaining from effort, passive, tame";
(ii)    "acting without effort, unstrained, easy."

The former reinforces the notion of effort as involving activity; the second (more common) is usually employed in the context of skilled performance. This would seem to render Laban's use of "effort" in the field of work and other operations involving skill somewhat paradoxical. On the other hand, we imply that there *is* effort involved in all such cases when, as we often do, we qualify "effortless" with "seems." as for example in describing the dancer soaring high into the air. or the swimmer cleaving through the water. We recognise that there is considerable exertion, but appreciate it as being of just the right kind so that it *appears* easy.

Laban himself was aware that he was using the term "effort" in a somewhat unusual way in applying it in such circumstances, as becomes clear in a paper published posthumously, "The Rhythm of Effort and Recovery" (Part I, 1959a), but he justifies its selection on the ground that *all* movement involves the expenditure of some energy. And his whole thesis is that the nature of the effort involved in recovery is as important as that demanded by the exertion itself. In this context, where he engages in an examination of the terms "effort" and "recovery" as they function in ordinary language (in a manner almost in keeping with contemporary linguistic/philosophical tradition!), he virtually acknowledges the threefold implications of the former as set out above, but after defining "effort" as "the active exercise of any power or faculty," indirectly suggests that common usage is at fault in restricting its application to situations requiring vigorous or laborious activity.

The opening paragraph of *Effort,* however, with perhaps the exception of the last sentence, epitomises the non-specific use of the term and the seemingly all-embracing character of the idea it is used to express:-

The tremendous collective effort made by political and economic associations, nations, and the whole of mankind is evident today to everyone who reads the papers and listens to the radio. The struggle for the technical mastery of our environment fascinates the spectator to such a degree that the importance of individual effort is often forgotten. The success or failure of our striving to res- olve the difficulties of existence and to bring order and prosperity out of chaos depends primarily on the personal contribution of millions of people to a common aim. Few people realise that their contentment in work and their happiness in life, as well as any personal or collective success, is conditioned by the perfect development and use of their individual efforts. We speak about "industrial effort," "war effort," "cultural effort," without realising that each collective action is built up from mental and manual efforts of individual people. We forget that all our striving to be reasonable and friendly and to combat our wrong habits are so many instances of individual effort. But what effort really is and how this essential function of man could be assessed and adapted to the specific necessities of life remains for most people an unsolved problem.

So far then (as well as in the next few paragraphs, in which similar general references to effort occur), the idea is, on the whole, little different from that suggested by a dictionary definition of the word. Webster, for instance, gives "the exertion of power, physical or mental," and for "exertion," under the same heading, "the vigorous exercise of any power of mind or body."

Only gradually does it become evident that this attempt "to penetrate to the core of man's effort" is from a particular angle, namely, the study of human movement. After allusions to methods of "effort assessment" and "effort control" worked out by the authors with people in industry (which are seen as "shedding a new light on the nature of effort"), the assertion is made:-

A person's efforts are visibly expressed in the rhythms of his bodily motion.

Later, however, there is reference to "the hidden effort behind the rhythm of movement and sound."

Already a certain ambiguity begins to be apparent, and this persists and indeed grows in complexity throughout this book, as well as in Laban's subsequent writings on the subject. On the one hand, "effort" seems to refer to physical activity which is observable; on the other, it sounds as though some occult mental faculty is being postulated which lies behind the overt movement which reveals it. It might even look as if Laban subscribes to the idea of the mind which derives largely from Descartes and which Ryle (1949) has called "the ghost in the machine." The frequent use of the somewhat indeterminate word "inner," and references to, for example, "this essential function of man," and "the core of man's effort," as well as statements such as:-

What has been taken so far as the basis of examination and test was but the surface indication of effort, not the effort itself

provide ammunition all too readily for anyone who wishes to charge Laban with being a victim of the Cartesian myth.

Part of the purpose of the first section of this essay is therefore to disentangle the various ways in which he uses the term "effort" or "efforts," and first it is proposed to look at those which do *not* seem to suggest a dualistic position, beginning with its application in respect of any kind of energy manifestation.

In Chapter V II it is used even in relation to machinery:-

Machines hit, press, lift, carry, smooth, flick, dab, wring, and so on, like a man, but machines can mostly exert one effort-action only, though in an intensified way.

Though this later is qualified ("the effort of the machine is in reality an artificial extension of man's effort"), the tendency to carry over to inanimate objects the use of a word which, as we have seen, properly refers to the activity of human beings and animals, is not exceptional.

It is evident again, for instance, in *Modern Educational Dance* (1948) in connection with the analysis of the eight "basic effort actions." In the chapter "Rudiments of a Free Dance Technique" each "effort action" is examined in some detail from various points of view, and then one particular "effort element" of that compound is singled out for special consideration, and there is always a short paragraph beginning "Physically, . . ." in which attention is drawn to some object or natural phenomenon which is regarded as exemplifying it. Thus, in the case of "thrusting" and "floating," for example, "suddenness" and "sustainment" are the elements respectively picked out, and the released jerk of a spring is contrasted with the hovering of smoke. Of course it might be argued that such descriptions are intended as analogies, that they are nothing more than a simplified (even an over-simplified) introduction to the whole subject. Obviously Laban was not the first to recognise that movement may be described in terms of its spatial, dynamic and time components (the factor of flow is another matter). Nor did he suppose that he was. But he must have been aware, as no doubt we all are when we try to help people to look at movement in terms of its constituent elements, that many, probably the majority, find it very difficult at first to do this, the tendency being rather to think of movements, items of behaviour such as getting up, closing a door, scratching one's head, and so on.

The other possibility, however, which cannot be overlooked in any attempt to explain these otherwise puzzling references to something which, in the main, comes to have psychological connotations, is that they illustrate Laban's apparent readiness to ascribe "effort" to practically the whole of the natural world, inanimate as well as animate. It then turns out to be the equivalent of some Life Force pervading the whole universe, in which case the whole idea becomes impossibly metaphysical, a version of panpsychism in fact, and the term is stretched to such limits as to lose any useful purpose.

Although in the course of this inquiry no instances have been found of "effort" being employed in contexts where Laban speaks in this vein, it is not inconceivable that the whole concept is to some extent bound up with a mystical belief in some sort of "driving power" or "rhythmic impulse" as animating all natural creation and reflected in man's movement as much as in any other kind (see, for example,

Laban, 1959b). And it would seem more than a coincidence that speculations about "life-powers," as in *Mastery of Movement on the Stage* (1950), are couched in language similar to that encountered in his exposition of "effort." For example:-

> These powers, or forces, have no names in our modern vocabulary, but we all know them when we meet them in the form of unaccountable inner drives, attitudes, emotions . . .

(In connection with this it is perhaps little wonder that students selecting topics for special study connected with "movement in nature" often find themselves in difficulties when they try to attribute to clouds, waterfalls, flames, and the like, "effort elements" of, for example, "fine touch," "flexibility" or "free flow." If these are to be used as technical terms descriptive of movement components expressing an "inner attitude," if they are to be recorded by signs which by convention indicate the nature of the "effort" made, then to apply them to rocks and stones and trees, etc., is to do something quite different from speaking of the *kinaesthetic response such phenomena may arouse in a human being.* It is to indulge in anthropomorphism, to imply that these things have intentions, strive for some goal, succeed or fail!)

"Effort" as bodily movement    To pass on now to less exceptional circumstances in which the word is used, i.e. where it seems to refer to *bodily exertions*, and particularly to the qualitative changes that occur within them. Since Laban's thesis is that the efforts we make are manifest in the rhythms of our bodily motion, that is, are perceptible either audibly or visibly (or both), it is hardly surprising that he is apt to use "effort" or "efforts" interchangeably with these manifestations themselves. We could often substitute the word "movement" or "movements," or a phrase such as "the rhythmic elements of movement" without any detriment (and sometimes to the improvement) of the sense. To take just one example. When the possible effect of repeated movements on the mood of a worker is being discussed, an instance is given of "regularly recurring violent contractions of the muscles of hands and arms," and it is then stated that "similar efforts are the expression of anger, impatience and even fury" (Laban & Lawrence, 1947). Obviously here "efforts" refers to something publicly observable, the physical movements themselves.

It is, indeed, *muscular energy* that the term often seems to describe in the early chapters of *Effort*. There is talk, for example, of workers using *too much* or *too little* "effort," which could hardly refer to anything other than force; moreover such allusions occur alongside those to much or little "strength." (Once again such usages might be accounted for as ways of introducing more complex aspects of the theory.)

However, it is the *eight "basic effort actions"* that we find most often referred to simply as "efforts" or even "the efforts"; and if one compares the two editions of *Modern Educational Dance* (1948 and 1963), or *Mastery of Movement on the*

*Stage* (1950), with the revised edition *Mastery of Movement* (1960), it will be found that in order to eliminate confusion on this point, Ullmann has consistently replaced "efforts" with "effort actions" whenever it is clear that it is Weight-Time-Space compounds that are being spoken about.

Certain ambiguities remain nevertheless in respect of "free flow" and "bound flow." Usually these elements are considered as aspects of "effort" (indeed Laban speaks of "flow effort" as he also speaks of "weight effort," "time effort," and "space effort"), but sometimes they seem to be set apart from it and even to stand in contrast to it. In *Effort,* when the factor of flow is first mentioned and is shown to constitute the nature and degree of control, for instance, we read:-

> Whether the right or the wrong movement is used depends upon the instinctive or conscious selection of effort, which must not be confounded with the control of the movement during action.

And in at least two practical classes in 1957 (the year before his death), Laban directed a sequence of movement (a "standard" or "primary" scale, to be exact*), in which alternate segments of the chain required, as he put it, "effort," and the other "flow".

It is not suggested that all of these uses are of equal importance, and some occur relatively infrequently; they have been explored chiefly in order to show that the term often refers to outward physical movement or to particular features of it which are publicly visible. By contrast, descriptions of "effort" as an "inner function" will now be examined.

*"Effort" as an "inner impulse"*

It is in this sort of language that, challenged to give an immediate answer to the question "What is 'effort'?" (or, more precisely, "What do you understand by Laban's use of the term 'effort'?"), many students of movement would be likely to couch their replies, perhaps speaking too, as Laban himself does, of "inner attitude" and "inner impulse." His well-known answer to his own question, "From where does the impulse of motion come?" is given as follows:-

> The impulse given to our nerves and muscles which move the joints of our limbs originates in inner efforts. (Laban, 1948).

Another passage in which Laban provides a definition of "effort" is to be found in *Mastery of Movement on the Stage* (and here we have a clear departure from standard usage), when he writes:-

---

*cf. *Choreutics* chapter VII.

In order to discern ("distinguish," 1960) the mechanical motion of ("from," 1960) living movement in which purposeful control of the mechanical happening is at work, it is useful to give a name to the inner function originating the movement. The word used here for this purpose is *"effort."* Every human movement is indissolubly linked with an effort, which is, indeed, its origin and inner aspect.

Here it is important to notice that the idea of intention is clearly written into "effort"; "purposeful control" could hardly be more explicit. And in contrasting in this passage the motion of a stone falling into a fire with a person falling and trying to avoid doing so, Laban is rightly insisting that human movement cannot be satisfactorily explained in mechanical terms alone, because it is not governed wholly by external forces operating on the body. So in this context "effort" is definitely not applicable to inanimate objects, but only to creatures capable of making decisions and choices.

If, however, there is talk of "origin" and "result" this suggests two things, or rather, two events or processes, one "inner" and one "outer" as they are regularly described; and in speaking in this way Laban becomes well and truly enmeshed in that most persistent and seemingly recalcitrant of problems which has exercised the minds of philosophers and others for centuries, that of the nature of the mind, and its relationship (if indeed there can be thought to be one) with the body. It is hardly surprising therefore that he is in deep waters when he tries to describe such a relationship, let alone explain it, through the notion of "effort," and his attemps are often seemingly contradictory.

In general he seems to adopt a frankly dualistic position but there are times when what he has to say seems more in accord with either a behavioural or an identity thesis. Although there are occasional uses of the compound noun "body-mind" in Laban's writings, and in *Effort* a reference to "bodily-mental effort," and though he might well have been expected to say "It is all one and the same thing," it is not at all clear that he could have thought this literally to be true. For this to be so, he would have been obliged to hold either a "mentalistic" or "idealistic" kind of view (which seems unlikely), such as that of the eighteenth century philosopher Berkeley, that only minds exist and that matter, and in particular bodies, do not, except in the mind; or else some kind of "materialistic" view whereby so-called mental events (thinking, having emotions, perceptions, sensations, desires, and so on), are conceived of as wholly physical occurrences. This again seems unlikely when we examine the way in which Laban constantly refers to mind *and* body, physical *and* mental, rather than in terms which imply that one can be reduced to the other.

As far as traditional body/mind theories are concerned, there are occasions when he seems to subscribe (even if unknowingly) to what is called the "double aspect" theory, which states that mental and physical phenomena are simply *different facets of the same thing.* The trouble with this account is that in trying to dispel one mystery it raises another; there are no longer two "things" to account for, but three! For what is it of which there are two aspects?

More often than not, however, a commitment to "interactionism" seems obvious. This, as the name implies, holds that body and mind *interact*. Over and over again movement is described as a two-way process—indeed Laban's whole account of the significance of human movement and of the importance of this for education rests firmly on a belief in the reciprocal influence of mental and physical activity. And a causal connection is clearly postulated when "effort" is specifically referred to as the *source* of which movement is the *result:*-

> The different activities of the child ... always have the same common result—movement—and the same common source—effort (Laban, 1948).

Similarly, in "The Rhythm of Effort and Recovery" (Part I, 1959a) he speaks explicitly of "the effort invariably preceding any movement," while "exertion" is held to be "a result of an effort."

As regards the "outer-inner" direction, we find frequent allusions to, for example, "the impact of movement on the mind," "the important effect action has on the mental state of the mover," how "movement can inspire accompanying moods," and there is the emphatic assertion:-

> It cannot be stressed too strongly that the movements the child experiences have a marked reaction on his mind, so that varying emotions can be induced through his actions, the intensity of the emotion varying with the intensity of the action. Small movements of the face and hands, or of isolated parts of the body, are as expressive of the child's mental state, and have as much effect on his mind, as larger movements, such as those carried out in an active lesson. (Laban, 1948.)

Conversely, the "inner-outer" direction is exemplified in the very notion of "effort" as "an inner impulse originating movement"; and there is his metaphor (1957) of the crane (the body) in which "sits a master mind, the crane-driver, who organises the motion of the crane ..." (which could hardly be nearer to an exact description of "the ghost in the machine").

The puzzling thing here, however, is what Laban says next:-

> We can know all about every single screw and pulley of the crane without being able to drive it by our thinking only. For the driving we need movement.
> The body is crane and crane-driver in one well-assembled unit, and this unit follows—knowingly or unknowingly—the invariable rules of bodily and mental motion.

Leaving aside the difficulties of the idea of "invariable rules," the question we may be prompted to ask here is whether Laban is perhaps leaning towards yet another theory (one which is a version of materialism in fact), that mental phenomena are *one and the same thing* as states and processes of the body, more specifically neurological events, even of the brain alone. This "identity" thesis, which is currently the most seriously discussed within this group of problems is, of course, totally incompatible with dualistic accounts of the Cartesian variety which have been almost completely abandoned in modern philosophical thought. *

It would be in accordance with such a theory that we could make sense too of Laban's talk of, for example, "the inner movements of thinking and feeling," "the effort-rhythm components of the human mind," and of "the rhythmic energy used in both mental and manual work" being the same. On the other hand, of course, as in cases where we speak of the mind wandering, leaping ahead, going round in circles and the like, all this could be construed as merely figurative description. This is typical of Laban's style in general and highly appropriate for some of the ideas he explores, but decidedly unhelpful if we are looking for *explanations,* which we are led to expect when he claims to be establishing scientific principles. So pictorially does he write that for the reader it often becomes difficult not to imagine the mind as a place, in which "efforts," as independent entities, bustle to and fro with almost a life of their own. He (1950) speaks, for example, of man's "inner world of efforts, which surge within his mind and find an outlet in the decision to move and to act " and of "the inner maze of the continuous flow of his intentions to move and to act."

But if Laban does sometimes seem to entertain ideas akin to the identity theory, it is difficult to make sense of his concepts of the "inner attitudes" of "fighting" and "indulging" which are said to characterise the nature of "effort." This could hardly be a description of brain states or events. It is also hard to see how he can maintain (1948) that "some people may never have experienced *either bodily or mentally* some of the efforts described here" (my italics). This indeed gives rise to all sorts of perplexities, since even if the term "mental" is to be taken as "intellectual" (a point to be considered later), it is not sense to say that we can make an effort without engaging in mental activity. If it is being suggested that twitches, reflex actions and other movements which we *cannot help* are "efforts" the concept is turned on its head. This is not only to subtract from it any idea of activity, intention or striving, but to legitimise the application of the term to the movements of a newly-decapitated chicken and the like!

On the other hand, it is perfectly good sense to say that mental effort (using the word as in common speech), may occur in the absence of outward movement. Although a good deal of mental activity is revealed in what we do or say, not all our ponderings and passions are manifest in publicly observable behaviour. They can remain invisible as well as silent, and we ourselves be the only ones who know

---

* For useful introductions to theories of the body-mind relationship, see Hospers (1967) and Shaffer (1968).

anything about them. However, it seems clear that such activity is *not* what Laban counts as "effort." In a discussion (1947) of rest and relaxation, a firm distinction is drawn between the two:-

> Rest is something else than relaxation, as in rest all effort is absent, while in the activity of relaxing some effort is present.

And though in *Modern Educational Dance* a more cautious statement is made to the effect that "rest might be considered as relatively effortless," the kind of effort in question seems to refer to scarcely perceptible movements such as those of breathing, rather than to mental activity such as listening attentively to a piece of music while lying motionless, or similarly concentrating in an intensely active manner, yet in complete stillness, on certain memories, images, problems, and so forth. By contrast, and surprisingly, in view of the declaration that "effort" is concerned with "purposeful control of the mechanical happening," the movements of a person who is asleep are seen as "effort" manifestations. In *Effort* we read:-

> A man must be dead or fainting if no effort-assessment on a motoric basis can be made of him. Even in sleep there are motions, for in any living being there is always breathing which is a continuously observable form of motion of variable effort-content.

One of the factors which undoubtedly contributes to this lack of clarity is Laban's varying use of the term "mental." On some occasions this is employed as in everyday speech as the adjective deriving from "mind" and in contradistinction to "physical"; sometimes, though never explicitly, it seems to be applied to what are, in fact, bodily processes, i.e. activity of the brain or of other parts of the nervous system; and finally, but not infrequently, it is used in place of "intellectual" or "cognitive." Thus we find it regularly opposed to, or at least juxtaposed with, "emotional"—an erroneous distinction which is apt to have unfortunate implications for his account of "educational" dance (see Essay C, Part 2a).

The term "mental effort(s)," however, sometimes has a special function, referring specifically to what is judged to be chiefly involved in the sort of activity in which non-manual workers engage, as contrasted with the "bodily" or "manual" kind, which is considered to be characteristic of workers performing operations requiring gross motor activity (see, in particular, *Effort,* pp. 60-64). Such a distinction, which raises the question of what is to count as "thinking," might well be judged too crude and arbitrary, reflecting the outmoded view that this is confined to abstract intellectual activity, what is done "with one's head," so to speak, and is not exemplified also in skilled performances with one's hands (or, for that matter, with one's feet, etc.), even though the former might be thought to constitute the paradigm.

Laban does not, however, suggest that "mental effort" is not also exerted and revealed in manual operations. In contrast to his mention of experiencing "effort" either bodily or mentally, he (1948) actually states that "there is a mental effort involved in all activity"; and manifestations of "mental effort" are held to be of significance as much in "practical" as in "intellectual" pursuits, both in the factory or office and in the classroom. "Visual attention," for example, is regarded as "a mental effort," and the *kind* (or kinds) of attention, and of what are called "intention" and "decision," necessary for a particular job, are, according to this theory, analysable in movement terms and detectable in a person's performance.

What is of most relevance to this inquiry, therefore, is that these "mental efforts" are no less observable than the "bodily" sort, that is, in what Laban (1950) terms "shadow moves" (sometimes "shadow movements" or "shadow actions")— "tiny movements of muscles which have no other than expressive value," especially of the face and hands, and which are "precursors or accompaniments of exertions or relaxations" (Laban & Lawrence, 1947). This idea, as was indicated earlier, might well be found ultimately to be one of his most original and fertile, although regrettably there is little information about either its details or its development. Any adverse criticism of Laban's inconsistent use of the term "mental" is thus by no means to be taken as a rejection of the suggestion that "shadow movements" (which are often unconsciously performed, but consist of rhythmic and spatial patterns fundamentally similar to and describable in the same terms as those of the larger and deliberate kind) may be important clues to some forms of mental activity, especially in their relationships with other movements which may occur simultaneously, or precede or follow them. Indeed it seems evident that as well as in respect of working efficiency they could have considerable significance in the assessment of personality generally, in non-verbal communication in everyday life, and of course in acting and the study of mime. Any restriction of the term "mental" to "intellectual" in this connection is therefore to impoverish, as well as misdescribe, the whole idea.

What does emerge in this context is that whatever the ways in which "effort" is used, it *never* has application in Laban's writings to situations where there is no observable movement. As he himself remarks in *Mastery of Movement on the Stage*, if it were otherwise effort(s) could not be perceived by others. And if we recall his tendency to replace the word "movements" with "efforts" it may be seen that "mental efforts" sometimes means, in fact, "shadow movements," so that references to, for example, "roundabout mental and bodily efforts" become less unintelligible.

Furthermore, the notion of "mental effort" affords a partial explanation of the difficulties in which Laban becomes entangled, not only in his choice of terms, but in formulating a tightly-structured theory of "effort." He is apparently wanting to say both that "effort" is concerned with conscious purposeful movement *and* with that which is unconscious and unintentional. It is, however, not impossible to have both conceptions. The idea of unconscious drives for example is, as Freud has shown, far from absurd, and that our "shadow movements" might be in some way connected with these and with other aspects of our unconscious life is not beyond the bounds of possibility.* But failure to make clear these two seemingly incompatible ways ot speaking of "effort," and to indicate when he is thinking exclusively in terms of it being conscious and intentional, as if this were the whole story, accounts at least for some of the ambiguities and apparent contradictions in Laban's writings on the subject, especially in *Effort* and *Modern Educational Dance.* It is worth noting that in his later book, *Mastery of Movement on the Stage,* he states explicitly that "effort may be both unconscious and involuntary."

Nevertheless, serious difficulties remain, and in any attempt to evaluate the usefulness of the concept of "effort," a distinction needs to be made between its descriptive and its explanatory aspects. If by "an inner impulse originating movement" Laban means that there is always some sort of mental event (whether conscious and deliberate or not) which precedes and causes movement, it has to be recognised that this is an attempted *explanation* of what happens when we move for which there is simply no evidence. Indeed it is difficult to see how there could be. Whereas it can easily be established that an exclusively physical event produces mental effects, any experiment designed to bring about an exclusively mental change is practically inconceivable. In spite, therefore, of the dominance of Descartes' theory for three centuries, the absence of any good reason to confirm it has led to its demise in recent years. But like the old categorisation of mental phenomena on the model of basic faculties of either a cognitive or a volitional or an affective kind, each thought to be capable of functioning separately and independently (though sometimes, as in the case of "reason" and "passion" seen as in conflict with one another), the "mental cause" theory of action is obviously part of the tradition which Laban inherited, and we should not be surprised that he did think along these lines.

If, however, we dismiss the hampering notion of an "inner function" and take "efforts" to be observable compounds of classifiable movement elements (which, as has been shown, is how Laban does employ the term on some occasions), whether within large, clearly-defined bodily exertions or small, subtle "shadow movements," the value of his account for *descriptive* purposes is considerable. What he has achieved in this area might be summed up as follows:-

**First,** he has formulated a classification of movement elements which is of particular importance in the realm of dance and movement expression, the latter being taken to include both *logically expressive* and *naturally expressive* movement.† And through his "effort" notation Laban has provided an essential tool not only for recording this aspect of movement, but also for learning to

---

* This whole area is in need of extensive empirical investigation, particularly perhaps from the point of view of its potential relevance to questions of deception.

†cf. Essay C, part 2a, below

observe physical behaviour in terms of rhythmic/dynamic elements. In addition, the further analysis of these elements in the revised edition of *Mastery of Movement* (1960), which he was working on during the last years of his life, and which seeks to indentify what is observable over and above the measureable components of human movement, points up a distinction which is of considerable interest from the aesthetic point of view. Although the characteristics of "weightlessness," "momentariness," "narrowness," and so on, are described as "qualities of psychomatic experience," and indeed are labelled "movement sensations," they relate directly to movement as an art form, since although in reality the two are not to be divorced, it is necessary to distinguish the *physical properties* of movement from its *perceptual qualities* for purposes of aesthetic discourse.

Just as there are different ways of speaking about a picture, for example—on the one hand, about its material elements (pigment on canvas, etc.), and on the other, about such things as its depth, rhythm, tension, and such like, which are non-material, but nevertheless perceived, so there are different ways of describing movement (cf. Wollheim, 1968). To try to apply considerations of the second kind to situations in which those of the first are more relevant, and vice versa, is often one of the main mistakes characterising debates between dancers and physical educationists; they are, in fact, referring to fundamentally different things. Arguing, for instance, that a movement downward after a leap *cannot* be "bound" because the mover cannot control his descent is irrelevant in dance; the point is that it may *look* (as well as feel) controlled and restrained, just as his soaring upward may appear light and buoyant in spite of it requiring a powerful thrust from the floor and strong tension to maintain his position in the air.

It is with this "sheer appearance of things," to borrow a phrase of Susanne Langer (1953), that movement as an art is concerned—with the creation of an *image* which, as she says, "exists only for perception, abstracted from the physical and causal order."* Beardsley (1958) neatly summarises the difference:-

To speak of a sculpture (a painting, a piece of music, a poem, a dance) as an *aesthetic object* would be to speak of it in respect of its perceptual qualities; to speak of it as a *physical* object would be to speak of its other characteristics.

**Secondly,** Laban has shown how movement elements are combined in a variety

---

* This however, is not to share her view that the "mysterious powers" which operate in the dance "are not the physical forces of the dancer's muscles," or that "the more perfect the dance the less we see its actualities." Reid (1970) is right to insist that "one accepts her affirmations, but suspects her denials . . . . The total thing is physical movement *with* its new emergent quality which she calls 'virtual'. It is not a dualism: there is one single entity—a complex monism of two aspects, conceptually distinguishable but existentially and artistically inseparable."

of ways, comparable to mixtures of colours; and how, within a phrase of movement, these compounds are related by different kinds of transitions which are also classifiable. Thus our understanding of the whole area of rhythm in movement, particularly of *free,* as distinct from *metric* rhythm, is greatly enriched.

**Thirdly,** he has suggested ways in which training in this rhythmical aspect of movement may be systematically carried out in conjunction with bodily and spatial aspects, so that an increasing range of skill and expression is made available to the performer.

**Fourthly,** Laban has given an indication of how particular combinations of movement elements are correlated with certain states of mind, which are not adequately described by existing conventional psychological terms, but which can nevertheless be categorised. This could prove to be of value for both personal and interpersonal understanding and, as a result, to have important implications for education. (A more detailed discussion of these matters is pursued in Essay C, part 3 below.)

In connection with this last point, it might be noted that no commitment to any particular theory of the body-mind relationship is necessary for it to be recognised that there is a link between at least some aspects of what we *call* mental experience, and outward bodily movement. We can, for example, favour the identity thesis which, strictly speaking, is not a body-mind account at all, since everything is conceived of in terms of the physical, and yet appreciate the significance of bodily movement and what we *refer* to as thinking, feeling, and so on.

We may also, without subscribing to the idea of a causal relationship between mental and physical phenomena, appreciate that the connection between particular mental states and particular combinations of "effort elements" may well account for what is often referred to as "inner participation" or "involvement" on the part of the performer—that seemingly intangible quality which marks out "sincere" or "vivid" or "lively" participation in dance, drama or mime. This was something which immediately commanded the attention and interest of educationists in the early days of "modern dance" in schools, when they saw children vitalised and animated* when working with "effort" ideas.

In conclusion, it must be stressed that because something "works" in practice, this is no proof of the soundness of the theory attaching to it. But while we may decline to embrace Laban's "effort" theories without qualification, there is no reason why we should not take advantage of many of his recommendations, at the same time questioning some of the explanations which accompany them. It is nevertheless doubtful whether the retention of the term "effort" is helpful, especially in view of the many misconceptions and confusions associated with it,

---

* Acknowledgement of the value of training in what is largely "effort" technique has also come from the theatre. (See, for example, Joan Plowright's remarks quoted in Stephenson, 1959, and Hepton, 1970.)

and perhaps it would be preferable to adopt his expression "eukinetics," or some other, in order to demarcate the dynamic/rhythmic aspect of movement.

Unlike some spheres of practical endeavour, in which it does not seem to matter a great deal what kind of theories are held so long as beneficial results are obtained, education demands a clear rationale on the part of teachers for engaging in particular activities in particular ways. Because, therefore, Laban's "effort" theories provide the basis for much of his educational practice, it now becomes necessary to examine the implications which they have in this sphere. Since his view of education is that it is primarily concerned with the maintaining and perhaps restoring of "effort balance" and "effort harmony," these concepts must be investigated in detail, together with those of "effort training" and "effort development," in order that we can clarify what we are trying to achieve and the means we are employing to do so.

# B EFFORT

## PART 2

"Effort
Training"

The fact that Laban refers to effort as "an inner function," and also speaks of "effort capacity" and "effort training," is apt to suggest that he is claiming that there is some kind of mental faculty, presumably related to movement performance, which can be exercised and developed in the way that it used to be thought that the memory or the will could be trained.

It is an adherence to this kind of outworn faculty psychology that, for example, Carlisle (1969) accuses Laban of in his analysis of the concept of Physical Education, in which he expresses doubts as to whether skilled performance in relation to objects. as in work or sport, could be achieved by a form of training conceived of in terms of the four motion factors. As he says, empirical evidence is against the hypothesis of a general motor skill or factor; and as far as the part that "effort training" could play in the acquisition of "closed" skills, such evidence does not seem to be forthcoming.

To some extent the need to give such training within the context of the particular activity in question does appear to have been recognised by the authors of *Effort* (and of course it might be remembered that, written in 1947, this book preceded the time when investigations into skill acquisition were undertaken in this country in any comprehensive and systematic way). They say, for instance:-

> Training for a definite task will best be done on the object during the operation. Explanations concerning the relationship and proportionality of efforts given during work can be completed in short sessions of special bodily exercises without objects or tools, which should stand, however, in direct connection with the task.

It would seem from this that the practice of "effort" sequences without the use of implements and materials is being recommended as part of an *explanation* of what is involved, and it is quite clear from the paragraph preceding the one quoted that theoretical understanding on the part of the operator, as well as practical experience, is regarded as essential.

But a later statement is all too dogmatic in tone, and much too sweeping a claim

41

in the absence of convincing data:-

> It is obvious that a person who has learned to distinguish the feel of pressing and gliding in all their shades of intensity will be able to do the practical tasks in which transitions between these two efforts are involved incomparably better and easier than a person who has hitherto never experienced such feel consciously.

The difficulty inherent in the assumption that a person with a well-developed range of "effort" is thereby equipped to accomplish efficiently any task to which he turns his hand is highlighted by the following assertion:-

> It is in this way that the practice of free movements containing basic efforts and transitions between them can be a useful preparation either for a definite job or for a general increase and refinement of effort capacity.

As regards the first part of this claim, which implies that specific training with tools, etc. follows practice of "free movements," Laban and Lawrence may have a case, though essentially one to be settled empirically. But "a general increase and refinement of effort capacity" is precisely what is *not* sufficient in training for work skills and the like. Just as it is impossible to develop "the imagination" in a *general* way, or similarly to foster "critical thinking," "creative ability" or "powers of communication," so practical skill and "work effectiveness" of a universal, non-specific kind cannot be promoted. Indeed this is quite contrary to what "training" implies. As Peters (1966) has pointed out:-

> .. . . the concept of 'training' has application when a skill or competence has to be acquired in relation to a specific end or function or in accordance with the canons of some specific mode of thought, or practice. If it is said that a person is 'trained' the questions 'To do what?', 'For what?', 'As what?' are appropriate; for a person cannot be trained in a general sort of way.

An even more erroneous supposition is that "effort training" and in particular "action training" (i.e. practice of the eight "basic effort actions" and of transitions between them), fits an individual to cope with life in general:-

> The child, becoming acquainted with the fluent performance of many practically useful bodily actions in dance, receives thus a valuable preparation for all the activities of life.

This is even more apparent in Laban's (1952) paper "The Art of Movement in the School":-

> Action, not only as physical exertion but in its real sense, stands in the centre

of life . . . . Man's actions, which influence his own and other people's happiness, must be sound and harmonious. The logical consequence of this necessity is, that action study and action training by means of the art of movement has a central purpose to fulfil. . .

Both physical education and "language education," between which the art of movement is said to hold "a central position," are considered inadequate in this respect:-

Neither of the border subjects of physical and mental training in the forms cultivated in the schools of our day is able to fulfil the essential task of real action training . . . . The art of movement teacher will gladly put his knowledge of basic movement and dance in the service of physical education. He will also help with his experience of expressive gesture in spoken drama. But what he also feels and stresses is, that his possible contribution to education is not at all exhausted in this help given to other subjects. The main educational effect of the practice of the art of movement as a guide to the development of the child's and the adolescent's action life, is hardly even touched upon in these side-lines of other subjects.

(The implications of this for the understanding of Laban's concept of "educational" dance are explored in Essay C, below.)

All this, however, rests on the mistaken view that bodily movement is to be equated with action. We may, and often do, speak of "action" when what we are in fact referring to is physical movement (and to emphasise yet again, there is no reason why, in a particular field, we should not if we so choose employ such a term *technically,* so long as we make it clear that we are introducing, for convenience, a stipulative definition). But it is important to recognise that movement of the body as such does not constitute an *action* or an *activity* as usually understood.* Actions and activities involve considerations of means and ends and of the agent's intentions, and are therefore subject to criteria of correctness or efficiency. Bodily movement (and we may remind ourselves that Laban, 1950, holds that "every human movement is indissolubly linked with an effort") occurs, for example, in sleep-walking, delirium, reflex actions, and physical behaviour under hypnosis and the influence of drugs, as well as in trembling, stumbling, and so on. But these are hardly things that we *do.* They are not *deeds* which we undertake and pursue successfully or unsuccessfully; they are rather things which happen to us, which we cannot help, which we are not described as doing well or badly, rightly or wrongly, and for which we are not likely to be held responsible.

---

* For further clarification of "activity" see Griffiths (1965), and of "action," Melden (1964), Vesey (1967) and White (1968).

Movement is intelligible as action or activity only in relation to the context in which it occurs, and to how the individual conceives of what he is doing. The same set of movements, and even the same rhythms and patterns which a person produces in carrying them out, might occur in widely differing circumstances. Whether it be analysed in terms of items of physical behaviour (e.g. walking across a room), body mechanics, anatomical, physiological or kinesiological changes, or sequences of rhythmic and spatial patterns, bodily movement gives no information by itself of *what* someone is doing. Ayer's classic example (quoted in Dearden, 1968), of a man raising a glass of wine and taking a drink aptly illustrates the distinction. It could, he suggests, be any of the following:-

> ... an act of self-indulgence, an expression of politeness, a proof of alcoholism, a manifestation of loyalty, a gesture of despair, an attempt at suicide, the performance of a social rite, a religious communication, an attempt to summon up one's courage, an attempt to seduce or corrupt another person, the sealing of a bargain, a display of professional expertise ...

What *is* true nevertheless, is that whichever of these it turns out to be, the *manner* of carrying out such an act may reveal whether, for example, the person concerned performs it with care and consideration or impulsively, with or without determination, nervously or with confidence, and so forth. And this is precisely where "effort" analysis can play an important part. But because the "effort" content of movement *reflects* personality and states of mind, it does not follow that the practice of "effort" sequences will result in what someone does in any particular contingency being appropriate or competent. This depends on a great many factors, chief among which are the individual's beliefs and his understanding of the rules and standards relevant to the matter. It may be (and in Laban's view is) possible to assess through a study of a person's movement his capacity for action, i.e. for getting things done, for achieving things as distinct from dreaming about them, for bringing plans to fruition. He may well be right that someone constantly exhibiting what he calls "incomplete effort" (movement in which "only one or two elements are charged with inner participation") will be, as he (1950) says, "doomed to lifeless inactivity." But no amount of "effort training," or for that matter any other kind of movement practice, is going to ensure that an individual *will* go into action in a given set of circumstances, much less that if he does, what he achieves will be in keeping with the standards of efficiency or of correctness appropriate to the situation or activity in question.

It is apparent, however, from Laban's (1959c) talk of "effort poetry" and of "a sphere of perfect efforts" (which he conjectures might be related to "an ethical sphere of values" having "a real existence" that is "outside man's personal configurations,") that his notions of "effort," and indeed of movement and dance, extend far beyond what would normally be thought of in this connection. Like his "space harmony" theories (cf. Curl 1966, 1967a, 1967b, 1968a, 1968b, 1969), they seem to be rooted in metaphysical beliefs which render some of his writings abstruse and sometimes nonsensical to the ordinary reader. In his rapturous idealisation of movement and dance ("all our ethical ideals and ideas" he declares, "originate from the cultivation of movement by our ancestors"), the concepts of dance and of "effort," in so far as the latter relates specifically to movement, are strained almost to breaking point so that they become practically meaningless.

Thus "effort training" is not conceived of simply as a means of increasing bodily skill, and *"humane* effort," which is referred to briefly and obscurely in *Mastery of Movement on the Stage* (1950) seems, in spite of Laban's assertion to the contrary, inevitably to involve moral considerations. In *Effort,* too, it is clear that improvement in working efficiency from the point of view of accuracy, speed, output and so on, is not all, or even chiefly, what he was interested in through the application of his theories in industry. He appears to have been equally concerned with what he saw as the effect of working movements on the individual worker's personal well-being, and with people's attitudes to work in terms of their enjoyment, or otherwise, of the movement involved.

In the Preface (1947) it is perhaps not insignificant that almost always, alongside mention of "economic prosperity," there occur allusions to, for example, "contentment in work and happiness in life," "well-being," "peaceful intercourse," "the broadening of human relationships in private and communal life," and "the increased enjoyment of work through the awareness and practice of its rhythmic character." There is more than a hint, taking the book as a whole, and especially the last chapter, that someone happy in his work will be efficient, and vice versa. Indeed, speaking of his training of assessors in industry, Laban (1954a) states explicitly:-

> Their work is based on the consideration that the most efficient worker is the contented one and happiness at work will only arise if the worker—no matter whether manual or mental—is in a job which is suitable for him.

It might be objected, however, that there are some happy-go-lucky people who are thoroughly inefficient in their work and, conversely, plenty of quite competent workers who happen to dislike what they do for a living. Laban's answer would appear to be "Yes—but such people cannot really be happy, or not for long. They are not leading a balanced existence, and eventually the strain of their ill-adjustment to work will tell. Frustration and discontent, as well as inefficiency, are bound to result from a situation of square pegs in round holes." This is bound up with his concept of *"effort balance"* with which that of "effort training" is closely linked and which merits special attention at this point.

It is, of course, not unusual for physical skill to be regarded as involving economy of effort (in its usual sense), and for recovery from exertion to be recognised as possible not only by refraining from work, as in tea-breaks, rest *"Effort balance"* periods and the like, but also during the operation itself, i.e. through movement of a *balancing* or *compensatory* nature. It is widely acknowledged too that well-regulated rhythmic movement, which consists of the alternation of complementary elements, may reduce and prevent fatigue, and often gives a certain aesthetic satisfaction both to the performer and the observer. When such economy is studied in terms of weight, time, space and flow, recovery is seen to depend on producing "effort elements" which contrast with those demanded in the main part of the process. Hence, Laban's rejection of the antithesis between effort and recovery: effort (though not necessarily of an energetic kind) is *involved in* recovery.

Presumably, therefore, in the field of physical skill it could be demonstrated empirically whether a person who finds difficulty in achieving those balancing "effort" combinations which are a necessary compensation for certain sorts of exertions is, or is not, less skilful than one who can, especially if and when endurance is concerned. That they should be taken into account in the selection of a person for a particular job is the basis of the argument in *Effort* against following a straightforward matching procedure, once the requirements of the task and the candidate's abilities have been assessed. The authors contend that it could happen that someone might be better *not* employed in a job for which he seems to have exactly the right attributes, because frequent use of these might lead to a certain "lop-sidedness" which would not only render his work less efficient in the long term, but also be detrimental to his personal welfare.

Because of the connection between movement and personality, and the ways in which physical behaviour reflects psychological states, the notion of "lop-sidedness" is also of relevance in relation to mental illness. Bodily movement and posture are among the most obvious ways in which psychiatric disorders become manifest; in Laban's terms there is an exaggeration of certain "effort elements" (for example, excessive tension to the point of cramp, or by contrast, limpness and heaviness), together with an inability to use the opposite end of the spectrum or other appropriate transitions, and a lack of fluency in relating one combination with the next. Thus movement is often unco-ordinated and marked by abrupt, i.e. "disharmonious" transitions, and the flow may be restricted to such an extent that movement becomes difficult and the patient even immobile. He loses that capacity which Laban sees as typifying the healthy human being of balancing, or effecting *a dynamic interchange* between his "efforts." What is lacking is "not the stable balance of immobility, but the dynamic balance of a well-proportioned alternation in rhythmic function" (Laban, 1960b). A somewhat similar loss, though not nearly so pronounced or intense, may indicate inner conflicts of a less serious nature to which from time to time we are all subject to some extent. Hence the significance of "effort" study for actors and dancers in the portrayal of character, and of the hostility or sympathy between individuals, which Laban sees as a clash or harmony of differing "effort" patterns. The results of such "effort chemistry" are, he concludes, the very stuff of drama. (See *Mastery of*

*Movement on the Stage.)*

The suggestion that in times of stress or depression movement sequences consisting of smooth, or "harmonious", transitions can have a beneficial effect, soothing or bracing, relieving or stimulating, as the case may be, is not difficult to appreciate. But what would be less credible would be the idea that movement, however carefully suited to individual needs, could ever *of itself* restore or maintain psychic equilibrium. This again depends on a person's beliefs—on his estimation of particular events and circumstances, and how he views the world and his situation within it. Ultimately, he can be helped only by an adjustment of those beliefs. To try to alter his movement would be to put the cart before the horse. It might relieve, but cannot, without other measures, cure.

Simply to be free of mental illness, however, is not always considered an adequate criterion for psychic well-being; it may be thought necessary, but not sufficient. And so there is talk of "integration," "the balance of psychic forces," "self-actualisation," and so forth, and a search for positive rather than negative attributes and for ways of achieving them (cf. Jahoda, 1958). For Laban, of course, "the great integrator" (see his *Movement Concerns the Whole Man,* 1958), is movement, and his advocacy of dance in education is inseparable from his view of it as a means of "harmonising" the personality. The following is a typical statement:-

> Harmonious movement exercise gives an experience of the reconciliation between the often antagonistic inner trends of man . . . such exercise can have a lasting effect on the integration of personality (Laban. 1954b).

All this, however, raises enormous problems, even when fanciful speculations are not involved about a pre-established order of the universe with which man is enabled to be in tune through dance. (This idea of Laban is discussed more fully in Essay C, below.) For although society adopts certain standards for fixing some sort of level *below* which it is determined what is to constitute abnormality in human behaviour and human development (each society thereby reflecting something of its particular values), it is virtually impossible to decide what, *above* that level, is to count as "wholeness" or "integration."

When applied to people, the slipperiness, not to say emptiness, of concepts such as "balance" and "harmony" becomes all too apparent. For who is to say what is a "balanced" existence? What sort of individual would be an example of a "whole" person? How are we to recognise a "harmonised" or "integrated" man or woman if we meet one? Notions of this kind, which in Western thought date back to Plato, with his talk of the "harmony of the soul," are rarely given any determinate content. And in educational discourse, where similar references often abound, any justification of them as aims of education is usually glossed over or omitted altogether. Nor is this easily achieved even if some sort of specification is drawn up

of what is involved. For if, as is often the case in Laban's writings,*
"harmonisation" and "integration" of the personality come to be associated with
the contentment and happiness of the individual, there always remains the ethical
problem of the pursuit of happiness† summed up in Mill's (1861) famous dictum:-

> It is better to be a human being dissatisfied than a pig satisfied; better to be
> Socrates dissatisfied, than a fool satisfied.

Even further back than the Ancient Greek idea of "harmony" is that of "health"
as conceived of in the ancient Chinese art of movement, T'ai Ch'i Ch'uan, a system
of physical exercises designed to bring about harmonious and effective intellectual,
emotional and spiritual functioning, in which it is known that Laban was
profoundly interested (see Laban, 1954c). But a definition of "health" even at the
physical level is not without difficulties, and there is a notorious lack of agreement
as to what constitutes "mental health," let alone what could be meant by that of
the "spiritual" kind. Certainly the suggestion that *treating* and *curing* are the
business of an educator is fraught with problems (cf. Peters, 1964, and Bantock,
1967).

Ideas of "integration" and "balance" presuppose, moreover, differentiated
elements, and "effort balance" in relation to the "harmonisation" of the
personality is bound up with the theory (to which it seems, Laban adheres) of basic
mental faculties of thinking, feeling, and willing, which are seen as being frequently
out of harmony with one another, but which he believes are integrated in the act of
dancing. Statements about a "balanced effort-life," "effort harmony," and
"integrated personality" often occur alongside those deploring a lack of balance
between intellect and feeling. But such a sharp distinction is artificial. Almost
everything that we do involves an interplay of cognition (perceiving, believing,
knowing, remembering, etc.), of affection (having feelings, moods, emotions, etc.),
and of volition (having desires, motives, intentions, etc.). As Bantock (1967) points
out:-

> There is not a wide range of behaviour which is the result of either emotional or
> intellectual factors to the exclusion of the other; most of our conscious actions
> are likely to involve some measure of combination of the two.

In Reid's (1961) words, feeling and emotion are "the subjective accompaniments

---

* He speaks, for example, of some kinds of movement producing "harmonious or serene and
gay feelings and impressions," while others evoke "feelings and impressions of anger,
unhappiness and disharmony" (Laban, 1951); and of "happy group dance experience" leading
to "a lasting harmonisation of personality" (Laban, 1954b).
† The concept of happiness, and its inadequacy as an aim of education, are examined by
Dearden (1967).

of the cognitive experience of an objective world." (Further reference to this point, in connection with dance, is made in Essay C. below.)

There is, however, the possibility that what might also be implied by "effort balance" which is not wholly unrelated to what appears to have been its original sense (namely, the use of contrasting rhythmic elements within sequences of movement), and which is both meaningful and of value in education, is that "the well-proportioned use of a number of different efforts" of which Laban (1948) speaks is a factor to be taken into account in composing and evaluating dance as an art form. The merest hint of this is given in his early references in *Modern Educational Dance* to "efforts which are finely balanced with each other" which, he says, "gives an aesthetic pleasure, like the colour-scheme in a picture or the harmony of sounds in music." Though he is referring here primarily to the nature of the experience of children engaging in repetitive rhythmic activities, the notion of "effort balance" could be extended to embrace considerations of the dynamic interplay and rhythmic relationship of one movement to the next, or one phrase or one section with another, and so on. This is well-exemplified of course in traditional sonata and symphonic form in music, in which one of the key features is the contrast of intensity, tempi and duration of the various "movements": in short, the kind of rhythmic "balance" that any artist is to some extent always concerned with in his striving to achieve a coherent structure, whatever the medium within which he works.

In Laban's writings then "effort balance" does sometimes function as a purely descriptive term, particularly when he is referring to recovery from exertion, but it would seem more fundamentally to be connected with certain ideals, again chiefly of a metaphysical kind. For him the harmonious, healthy (and indeed virtuous) human being is one in whom a rich, ordered "effort development" has taken place, and since "thorough effort training can be achieved only through dancing," (1948) the dance, albeit in a far from usual sense of the term, is the highest order of activity, the supreme mode of existence. But if the dancer is one who lives and acts "in accordance with the great dance of bodily, psychic and spiritual phenomena that fills the whole world" (see Laban quoted in Ullmann, 1964), the ordinary teacher working away in school or college at his task of initiating others into what might generally be assumed to be an aesthetic discipline is hard put to it to know what relevance such ideas of "balance" and "harmony" have for him.

At this point, therefore, some consideration of Laban's concept of "effort development" and of his view of education is called for. **"Effort development"**

These, however, are somewhat problematical. Sometimes both seem to be regarded as self-effected, or even as natural processes, at others as essentially dependent on social influences. In many respects Laban belongs to the tradition of what has become known as "growth" theory, with an account of human development as a kind of "unfolding" or "inner ripening."* He (1948) speaks, for example, of "the spontaneous growth and blossoming of efforts" through dance, and reference to "the growth of efforts in number, intensity and refinement" is apt to suggest that "effort development" is conceived of as a straightforward evolutionary process characterised by multiplication, differentiation and integration. "Effort" thus sounds here like a name for some sort of biological entity or function, rather than something which a person engages in out of choice and for which he has responsibility. And a predetermined end-state which represents the culmination of the process is implied by the remark in *Mastery of Movement on the Stage* that "in both the life-history of the individual and of mankind progress is made towards all-round effort mastery" (in the 1960 edition, " . . . towards the mastery of effort balance"). The development of "efforts" of the "strong," "quick," "direct" kind, and later of the "light," "sustained," and "flexible" variety, which is postulated in *Modern Educational Dance,* also tends to suggest that a definite sequence is followed by all human beings, to which they cannot help but conform, irrespective of cultural and social norms. In the case of flow it is asserted that "this develops slowly, and in some cases never at all."

Some of Laban's thinking thus seems to be permeated by the belief that, given favourable conditions, there is a *natural* process of mental maturation which comes about much as in the case of that of the physical; though "effort development" does not sound like some ordinary physical process which just happens, such as the growth of hair, or the ability to focus the eyes. It seems rather to be something which the individual *strives to achieve,* even though, as Laban (1948) observes, "the aim is not known to the baby."† The idea that human development consists in a striving towards the perfection of which the individual is capable is, however, typical of many of Laban's generation, not least some who have had a marked influence on education in this century. It has, in fact, a long philosophical history, and the concept of "effort development" is in certain respects not unlike that of Spinoza's notion of "endeavour" or the tendency of everything "to persist in its own being." (The similarity in the choice of term is, of course, striking.)

On the other hand, throughout Laban's writings there is a marked insistence that the "effort characteristics" of human beings not only become enriched and differentiated in the course of general development, but may be changed and organised in particular ways for particular purposes. In *Effort* the contention is that in the interests both of efficiency in work and of living in general, "it is fundamentally the awareness that man can check and alter his effort-rhythms

---

* On "growth" theories in education see, for example, Dearden (1968).

† In his discussion of the baby's development from the rolled-up position of the foetal state it may be noted that, though the idea of intention is lacking, the term "effort" has here its usual connotations as regards activity, not passivity, and also of struggling to overcome some condition or obstacle.

which is needed." If it were otherwise, of course, Laban's theories of "effort training" would be meaningless.

This fact is what Laban sees as a basic difference between humans and other animals. Human "effort characteristics," he holds (1950), are not only more varied than those of animals, but also much more variable. Further, "man is the only living being who is aware of and responsible for his efforts." As well as establishing (in the words of the 1960 edition of *Mastery of Movement*), "complicated networks of changing effort qualities," human beings have "the capacity to comprehend the nature of the qualities, and to recognise the rhythms and structures of their sequences." It is thus that there is "the possibility and the advantage of conscious training."

It would therefore appear that, like the somewhat ambiguous term "child development," "effort development" is open to different interpretations, or perhaps seeks to embrace two different ideas. It may refer *either* to a natural process, governed by scientific laws and therefore subject to investigation along observational lines, *or* to a process of change susceptible to personal and cultural influences in the light of particular purposes and selected ideals. In the case of the former, much more needs to be known about children's developing rhythmic capacities. If the latter construction is put upon it, "effort development" approximates to "effort training," taking this to imply increasing mastery of the rhythmic/dynamic elements of movement. It therefore becomes of interest to the educator. But it is essential to be clear about the particular goals towards which "efforts" are to be directed, along with the standards characteristic of the activity in question. Sheer multiplicity is not enough. Presumably it would be possible to have a wide "effort" range, but use it for all sorts of undesirable or trivial purposes, such as tormenting animals or wriggling one's scalp, and fail to select and organise it appropriately either in the aesthetic realm or in situations demanding efficiency. The development of "efforts" cannot occur in a vacuum, but must take place within a specific context, and if the aim is to achieve skill in some practical task it will be undertaken in a manner different from that employed in relation to the practice of movement as an art form.

In connection with the latter, a point of considerable importance arises as a result of Laban's view of artistic activity as a special branch, as it were, of "effort cultivation." Man, he (1950) says, " has broadened the scope of effort-training into the creation of works of dynamic art." And because the qualities of movement reflect his inner life, he is enabled, through the ordering and arranging of these qualities (as in dance), to become conscious of states of mind of which he is otherwise not aware. Laban does not state the case precisely in these terms, but it seems a not unreasonable interpretation of some of the things he has to say. In particular, in his first reference in *Mastery of Movement on the Stage* to "movement thinking" (later this becomes something slightly different, applying simply to considering movement in terms of weight. time, space and flow), he would appear to be reflecting along these lines. The following, when looked at from this point of view, is not only of interest in relation to the debate in aesthetics about works of art and their authors' intentions but, for this reader at any rate, gains in intelligibility:-

> Movement-thinking could be considered as a gathering of impressions of the happenings in one's own mind, for which nomenclature is lacking. This thinking . . . perfects man's orientation in the inner world of efforts, which surge within his mind and find an outlet in the decision to move and act.
>
> Man's desire to become orientated to the inner maze of the continuous flow of his intentions to move and act results in definite effort-rhythms, as practised in dancing and mime. *

Similarly, his reference (1948) to dance as "a language of action in which the various intentions and bodily mental efforts of man are arranged into coherent order" takes on a new significance when viewed in this way.

If this interpretation is correct, the implications for a re-assessment of the value of movement as an art are considerable. *Just as we require language to make available to us the kind of thinking which is expressible in words, so through movement symbols a different realm of thought and feeling is opened up which is peculiar to movement.* A common assumption is, of course, entirely the reverse. It is often supposed that we first have an idea or some affective experience, and then express it in language or translate it into bodily action or some other symbol. But without the relevant symbol (or, in some cases, a sign or an image), the mental experience itself is not within our reach at all. Something of what Hirst (1966) has to say about language and thought is pertinent in this connection, even though in the art symbol there is always an ambiguity of meaning.

> Nor when we look for words in which to express what we want to say, is it the case that we have the precise thought in ideas which we cannot adequately code. Rather it is that we have not yet got the appropriate thought because we have not yet formulated it in words. Surely we only have a particular thought if it is formulated in relevant terms, for to have a specific thought is to entertain a set of symbols that have that specific meaning (Hirst, 1966).

While language has always rightly held a foremost place in education, the arts are much less likely to be regarded as a means of *developing* thought and feeling. No doubt the expression and communication theories of art, dominant in the West in recent decades, largely accounts for this; but Wollheim, stressing the close

---

*Laban seems to attach a rather special meaning to "mime," which he (1950) describes as "expressive of effort, and a fundamental activity of man." What he is at pains to emphasise is that it involves "the avoidance of the simple imitation of external movement-peculiarities."

connection between aesthetics and the philosophy of mind, gives prominence to the idea that through his creations the artist becomes acquainted with states of consciousness which are not otherwise knowable:-

> If someone can recognise in something that he's made a reflection of an inner state, it is often the case that he would not have been aware of this state except through the object or objects that he makes. And an explanation of this can be that the mental state or condition, though in one sense remaining unchanged, has acquired or developed a structure, a degree of inner articulation that it previously lacked (Wollheim, 1971).

Laban's suggestion (1950) that "the repeated exercise of effort-configurations prevailing in the action-thinking of a community results in the creation of tribal or national dances," which epitomise "the states of mind or traits of character cherished and desired within a particular community," is perhaps not so very far removed from Wollheim's contention that art is concerned with

> aspects of the mind which have to do with the development, with the emergence, of the mind, or the way in which we come to acquire self-consciousness, or our conception of ourselves as persons,

nor from his proposal that through the creating of a work of art "the person comes to recognise what he is like . . ." (There is, of course, an important difference here in respect of *individual* and, as it were, "collective" personality.)

What is crucial in Wollheim's argument, however, is that the artist's activity is conscious and intentional; he knows what he is doing, he understands his medium and the techniques involved in creating in that medium, and he already possesses some concept of, for example, a poem or a carving. Indeed the process of *clarifying* and *structuring* is indispensable both in respect of the material with which he is dealing, and of the "mental state" (which Wollheim implies is not exactly a satisfactory term in this context) which it matches. It is here that certain aspects of Laban's account of "effort" in relation to dance and education raise serious difficulties. For an understanding of structure, and the ability to create structured wholes, is not something which occurs fortuitously or by the light of nature, but is achieved through acquaintance with examples of created forms, and by a process (often long and arduous) of active learning, usually under the guidance of those who have already gained such mastery in the particular field in question.

Yet from the way in which Laban speaks on some occasions, it is apt to sound as if education (institutionalised education, that is, as distinct from self-education), is really something of an unfortunate necessity in a society which mars, or at least makes for hindrances to "nature." And dance tends to sound like an activity which the individual almost instinctively pursues, or at most picks up, rather than learns, a ready-to-hand means of attaining harmony that preserves and strengthens the rich

"Effort" and education

store of efforts with which Laban believes all human beings to be initially endowed. ("The full range of typical effort-tendencies has been inherited"—by men as well as by other animals, we are told in *Mastery of Movement on the Stage.)* Many instances might be cited which suggest that Laban views the conditions of an industrialised environment as frustrating an innate drive towards natural harmony, and that if only we lived a "natural" existence and danced as primitive man danced all would be well with our "effort life"—with, indeed, Life!

There is more than a touch of Rousseau's "noble savage" ideal in Laban's thinking, and in a discussion (1950) about changes of style in social dancing he writes:-

> It is probable that what is called period style is mostly the fashion of the well-to-do minority of a community at a specific historical era, while the natural behaviour of the majority has changed very little throughout the whole history of mankind. This natural behaviour was determined at all times by a broad range of action-efforts occurring in everyday working life, and is the natural movement expression of emotional and mental states.

Children too, like the pre-industrial worker with his festive folk-dances arising from pride in work of a non-specialised kind which provided him with "a rich movement life," are regarded as having "a natural effort-richness"; and it is Laban's view that the main concern of movement education is to keep this alive and flourishing.

It is true that, with young children, movement indulged in for its own sake, such as rhythmically repetitive stamping, jigging up and down, clapping hands, spinning round and so on, is of a dance-like character. Laban is probably right that movement play of this kind is "the great aid to growing effort-capacity and effort-regulation," if this is taken to mean an enlarging of the range of rhythmic/dynamic movement and increasing its control. And it seems sensible for the educator to take advantage of this delight in rhythmicised and patterned movement, which fulfils no practical purpose, as a basis for initiation into the art form of dance. But it is no more than a beginning. Of itself it does not constitute artistic activity (though it may, for the observer, have aesthetic elements within it, the aesthetic being a wider concept than that of art), and it does not lead automatically to the making of dances. For a created whole to emerge more than spontaneous "prancing," to use of term of Sachs (1937), is necessary. As Reid (1969), discussing the question "Is it 'art' that children do?" and examining the nature of young children's explorations in the field of drawing and painting, puts it:-

> These rudimentary experiences can have an aesthetic quality; but they are not 'art' in any serious recognised sense. 'Art' seems to imply some measure of intention, at least in a loose sense of the word—intention to make and give form to something; it involves some element of self-criticism: if the thing is not

quite right, it must be altered or modified or done again better.

And later:-

> We learn to do new, creative things not by 'first' but by 'second nature'. We learn how to *become* 'natural', to acquire a new kind of spontaneity through passing through stages of hard discipline.

Dance as art then is not some sort of natural phenomenon, a slice of ordinary everyday behaviour. What Laban considers as *educational* dance, however seems to be rather different from the *art* of dance. Though he (1950) states that the "efforts" of children and of animals in their play "are intermingled in an almost casual and irregular way," whereas in dance "they are neatly selected, worked out, and separated," as far as education is concerned he seems to lean more towards a play account. Yet without guidance in such selection and structuring of "efforts" it is difficult to see how, by simply having a wide range, an individual could be considered *educated.* It would be rather as if he had a palette of infinitely varied and subtle colours, but no idea of how to use them discriminatingly, and no concept of a painting.

The creating of something of aesthetic value, and the attainment thereby of states of mind which bring an enlargement of self-knowledge, are not achieved under "natural" conditions in which a kind of all-round, undifferentiated "effort-exercise" occurs. It may be the case that ultimately no one can be *taught* to create an aesthetic object, but there are a great many things to be learned which assist in the process and which can be learned only in a situation where the concept of "art" is understood, and where there are opportunities to profit from those who have engaged in its practice and study.

To sum up the cluster of concepts associated with "effort":-  **Summary**

**First**, the notion of "effort training" is to be rejected out of hand if it is intended to imply that there is a general motor ability factor which can be exercised and developed so that efficiency in a variety of situations will result. This is not, however, to deny that the recognition of all movement as a composite of rhythms and shapes which can be broken down into simpler elements might assist, and even play an important part in the learning of specific techniques, *provided that* training along these lines is carried out in conjunction with other procedures peculiar to the operation in question. Indeed, it is usually in terms of the changing energy, time and space components of movement that trainers in movement of all kinds, from driving instructors to golf professionals, from cookery demonstrators to ski-ing experts, pass on their expertise (whether they are aware of it or not, and probably never having heard of Laban). Whether someone thoroughly familiar with "effort" technique and theory finds it easier and possibly more interesting to tackle new skills is clearly an empirical matter; but the question of whether he learns more effectively by this means than others trained along different lines is quite another issue.

"Effort training" then cannot be taken to mean the training *of* "effort," in the sense of some inner function, but must imply training *in* "efforts" in terms of the rhythms and qualities of movement, with special reference to their ordering and arranging and in relation to some specific end. This aspect of movement experience and understanding is obviously essential in dance, as well as having application in drama and mime.

**Secondly,** the concept of "effort balance" has similarly both negative and positive aspects. Where it is extended to the psychological make-up or state of the individual to imply a "harmonious" or "harmonised" personality, it can only be regarded as vacuous; it is a metaphysical notion traceable back to antiquity, implying a perfection of being which everything has potential to achieve, and towards which everything constantly strives. If, however, it applies to the way in which the rhythmic/dynamic elements of movement are arranged and organised either for the purpose of recovery from exertion or for aesthetic purposes, it has both content and relevance—in the first case, in circumstances where economy of energy is a prime concern, in the second, in relation to dance composition.

**Finally,** the concept of "effort development," if implying the growth of "efforts" as a natural process leading towards an ideal end-state of "effort harmony," is of a dubious character, deriving from a view of the human being as having a given "nature" which evolves along certain prescribed lines. What is insufficiently recognised here is the *social* nature of human learning and development. It is not only that the development of "efforts" in the sense of mastery of the rhythmic aspects of movement is of necessity effected in a social context, but that it is partly a reflection of that context. Whatever form it takes, from gliding smoothly over the ground to soaring lightly into the air, from stamping and hopping and whirling round and round to performing delicate movements with the fingers or executing complex step-patterns, it is a social achievement made possible for the individual by his being born into a society where people who have learned such things value them and pass them on to others.

Since the transmission of such skills and understanding by those already in possession of them is part of what is involved in education, it is clear that a satisfactory account of dance as an educational activity cannot be in terms of "efforts" developing *naturally.* But if the term "effort development" is to be interpreted much as it has been suggested here that "effort training" is to be interpreted, then it is clear that both through Laban's classification of "effort elements" and "effort compounds," and through his suggestions for ways of using these in relation to movement expression, the concept is not only meaningful but of value.

What is still necessary, however, is an inquiry into what sort of an activity it is within which the development of an individual's "efforts" is of prime importance. Since the logical status of modern educational dance is almost permanently in dispute (is it an aspect of aesthetic education or something else? What is its relationship with "the art of movement"? etc.) a detailed analysis of this concept is required. This is attempted in Essay C, below.

**References**

BANTOCK G.H. (1967) "Education, Culture and the Emotions". London: Faber & Faber.

BEARDSLEY M. (1958) "Aesthetics". New York: Harcourt, Brace & World.

CARLISLE R. (1969) The concept of physical education—I. In Proceedings of the Annual Conference, Phil. Educ. Soc. G.B.

CURL G.F. (1966) Philosophic foundations (Part 1). *L.A.M.G.Mag.*, **37**, 7-15.

CURL G.F. (1967a) Philosophic foundations (Part 2). *L.A.M.G. Mag.*, **38**, 7-17

CURL G.F. (1967b) Philosophic foundations (Part 3). *L.A.M.G.Mag.*, **39**, 25-34.

CURL G.F. (1968a) Philosophic foundations (Part 4). *L.A.M.G.Mag.*, **40**, 27-37.

CURL G.F. (1968b) Philosophic foundations (Part 5). *L.A.M.G.Mag.*, **41**, 23-29.

CURL G.F. (1969) Philosophic foundations (Part 6). *L.A.M.G.Mag.*, **43**, 27-44.

DEARDEN R.F. (1967) Happiness and education. In Proceedings of the Annual Conference, Phil. Educ. Soc. G.B.

DEARDEN R.F. (1968) "The Philosophy of Primary Education". London: Routledge & Kegan Paul.

GRIFFITHS A.P. (1965) A deduction of universities. In R.D. Archambault (Ed.) "Philosophical Analysis and Education". London: Routledge & Kegan Paul.

HEPTON B. (1970) Laban and the training of actors. In L.A.M.G. 'Kaleidoscopia Viva' Souvenir Programme.

HIRST P.H. (1966) Language and thought. In Proceedings of the Annual Conference, Phil. Educ. Soc. G.B.

HOSPERS J. (1967) "An Introduction to Philosophical Analysis". (Revised edit.) London: Routledge & Kegan Paul.

JAHODA M. (1958) "Current Concepts of Positive Mental Health". New York: Basic Books.

LABAN R. & LAWRENCE F.C. (1947) "Effort". London: Macdonald & Evans.

LABAN R. (1948) "Modern Educational Dance". London: Macdonald & Evans.

LABAN R. (1950) "Mastery of Movement on the Stage". London: Macdonald & Evans.

LABAN R. (1951) What has led you to study movement? *L.A.M.G. Mag.*, **7**, 8-11.

LABAN R. (1952) The art of movement in the school. *L.A.M.G.Mag.*, **8**, 10-16.

LABAN R. (1954a) The work of the Art of Movement Studio. *J. Phys. Ed,* **46**, 23-30.

LABAN R. (1954b) Letter to all Guild members. *L.A.M.G. Mag.,* **12,** 5-9.
LABAN R. (1954c) Laban lecture. *L.A.M.G.Mag.,* **12,** 22-25.
*LABAN R. (1957) Education through the arts. *L.A.M.G. Mag.,* **19,** 4-7.
*LABAN R. (1958) Movement concerns the whole man. *L.A.M.G.Mag.,* **21,** 9-13.
*LABAN R. (1959a) The rhythm of effort and recovery. (Part I). *L.A.M.G.Mag.,*
    **23,** 18-23.
LABAN R. (1959b) The aesthetic approach to the art of dancing. *L.A.M.G.Mag.,*
    **22,** 29-32.
*LABAN R. (1959c) Dance as a discipline. *L.A.M.G.Mag.,* **22,** 33-39.
LABAN R. (1960a) "Mastery of Movement" (2nd. edit. revised L. Ullmann).
    London: Macdonald & Evans.
*LABAN R. (1960b) The rhythm of effort and recovery. (Part II). *L.A.M.G.Mag.,*
    **24,** 12-18.
LABAN R. (1963) "Modern Educational Dance" (2nd. edit. revised L. Ullmann).
    London: Macdonald & Evans.
LABAN R. (1966) "Choreutics" (Ed. L. Ullmann). London: Macdonald & Evans.
LANGER S.K. (1953) "Feeling and Form". London: Routledge & Kegan Paul.
LANGER S.K. (1957) "Problems of Art". London: Routledge & Kegan Paul.
MELDEN A.I. (1964) Action. In D.F. Gustafson (Ed.) "Essays in Philosophical
    Psychology". London: Macmillan.
MILL J.S. (1861) "Utilitarianism". Republished (1962). London: Fontana Books.
PETERS R.S. (1964) 'Mental health' as an educational aim. In T.H.B.Hollins (Ed.)
    "Aims in Education: the philosophic approach". Manchester: Univ. Press.
PETERS R.S. (1966) "Ethics and Education". London: Allen & Unwin.
REID L.A. (1961) "Ways of Knowledge and Experience". London: Allen &
Unwin.
REID L.A. (1969) "Meaning in the Arts". London: Allen & Unwin.
REID L.A. (1970) Movement and meaning. *L.A.M.G.Mag.,* **45,** 5-31.
RYLE G. (1949) "The Concept of Mind". London: Hutchinson.
SHAFFER J.A. (1968) "The Philosophy of Mind". London: Prentice Hall.
STEPHENSON G. (1959) Laban's influence on dramatic movement. *The New Era,*
    **40,** 55, 98-102.
ULLMANN L. (1964) Laban and education through movement. *L.A.M.G.Mag.,*
    **32,** 20-26.
VESEY G. (1967) Conditioning and learning. In R.S. Peters (Ed.) "The Concept of
    Education". London: Routledge & Kegan Paul.
WHITE A.R. (1968) "The Philosophy of Action". London: Oxford Univ. Press.
WOLLHEIM R. (1968) "Art and Its Objects". New York: Harper & Row.
WOLLHEIM R. (1971) Talking about aesthetics. *The Listener,* **85,** 201-204.

---

*These papers are also in L. Ullmann (Ed.) "Rudolf Laban Speaks about Movement and
Dance." (1971) Surrey: Lisa Ullmann.

# C

# MODERN
# EDUCATIONAL
# DANCE

# C MODERN EDUCATIONAL DANCE

## INTRODUCTION

It is a common, though perhaps curious experience for the student (or teacher) of dance to find that mention of his subject is apt to prompt the question from the lay person, "What sort of dance do you study (or teach)?" Yet a similar query in respect of any of the other arts would appear somewhat odd.

True, there might well be inquiries about particular works or periods selected for special consideration as part of the historical aspect of these disciplines (it being assumed that this is an integral feature of the total study). But "What type of music?", "What kind of literature?" or "What style of painting?" is not usually asked of the student of music, literature, or art; it is recognised that there is the "substance," as it were, of music itself, of painting, sculpture, and so on.

There are probably several reasons for this discrepancy in the case of dance, not least the paucity of dance "literature," i.e. choreographic scores or records on film; but this is not the main concern here, though it will be maintained that the conclusions reached in connection with an inquiry into modern educational dance might have a bearing on the problem. The present aim is to try to clarify this latter concept, for the appearance of this phenomenon in the 1940's might seem to have added yet a further strand to the existing profusion of dance forms. In view of its widespread influence in colleges of education and many schools, but at the same time in the light of prevailing confusion about its precise nature and aims, this would seem to be a necessary step before the justification of dance as a curriculum activity can be attempted. It will nevertheless be argued that such a clarification is of some importance in providing that justification.

What, then, does the term "modern educational dance" imply? Is it meaningful at all? Does it refer to a brand, or a branch, of dance which is different from other kinds? And if so, what is distinctive of it?

We might note first that, like "effort," it is a technical concept; but unlike "effort" it is a term confined to educational discourse, and is not illuminated by reference to the way in which it is used in ordinary language (cf. p.2 above). It calls rather for a survey of the theory and practice involved, which, as is well known, spring directly from the work of Rudolf Laban. The expression "modern" is, however, of some significance in view of the connection between the activity in question and Modern Dance,* this being understood as a generic term embracing those forms of dance which owe their origins either to "la danse libre" of Central Europe (in which Laban played a leading part) or to the American pioneers Isadora Duncan and Ruth St. Denis. This connection† merits some attention in the course of this analysis; while "educational," carrying as it does the suggestion that other sorts of dance are *not* educational, or at least not so educational or perhaps *non*-educational, invites examination of whatever are found to be the distinguishing features of the subject in the light of specifically educational criteria.

It is therefore necessary, in order to have a frame of reference, to be clear at the outset regarding what is understood by "education," and throughout this essay the standpoint taken is:-

**first,** that education is a deliberate enterprise undertaken by one party in the interests of another, as distinct from self-education and informal processes (neither of which, of course, it is intended to suggest is unimportant, but both of which belong to concerns falling outside those of curriculum planning);

**secondly,** that it is centrally concerned with the development of individuals capable of choice and self-direction, and of ordering their actions in the light of rationally determined principles;

**thirdly,** that such development is a social achievement, available only to human beings brought up in a community of other persons;

**fourthly,** that this process involves the development of a differentiated understanding of experience, which is possible only through an initiation into the various modes of thought and feeling** that mankind has evolved throughout the centuries.

This is inevitably nothing more than a highly-condensed summary of some of the main requirements held to demarcate a concept which, in a complex and pluralistic society such as our own, is likely to be controversial and to some extent regarded as overlapping with others. It would obviously be inappropriate here to rehearse the arguments leading to a full analysis,†† but it is important to insist that for the concept to be at all a distinctive one, it is essential that education is not confounded with, for example, therapy, entertainment, or socialisation; though this does not, of course, rule out the possibility that education *may* have both preventative and curative effects, *may* prove to be enjoyable, and *may* (and indeed *must* in one sense, as already indicated,) function as a socialising force. As soon as it is conceived of as implying more than socialisation of the kind designed to secure the passing on of certain knowledge, practices, customs and ideals, and is taken to involve also the transmission of the attitudes and skills which make possible the

---

* For the purpose of distinguishing "Modern Dance" from "modern educational dance," the former will be indicated throughout by capital initial letters.
† See Layson (1970) for a more detailed discussion.

**cf.p.X above.
††See, for example, Peters (1966), Langford (1968).

challenging of such values, and when, moreover, special institutions are set up for these purposes, what is regarded as educative necessarily becomes more strictly, and consequently more precisely, defined.

It is further assumed for the purposes of this essay that among the differentiated modes of experience referred to above is *aesthetic* understanding, and although particular problems arise in conjunction with this because of the difficulty of establishing objective criteria within the various branches, it is nevertheless being taken for granted here that such a form of awareness is of educational value. If, therefore, modern educational dance is shown to be an aspect of aesthetic education, its claim to a place in the curriculum will be considered just. It is, however, precisely because some doubt exists as to whether it *is* to be regarded in this light that the concept requires examination.

Uncertainty on this point arises both in connection with the theory and practice of the subject, though in the years since its introduction into this country there has understandably been considerable variation in respect of what actually goes on in the name of this activity. This discussion will therefore be based chiefly, though not exclusively, on the exposition provided by Laban himself, his book *Modern Educational Dance* (first published in 1948 and revised by Lisa Ullmann in 1963)* being taken to serve as the principal focus of inquiry. Some reference will however also be made to authors known to base their practice on Laban's ideas, both as explicitly stated and as implicit in his own teaching and in that of others owing their inspiration mainly to him.

Although what may be regarded as the chief characteristics of modern educational dance are closely interwoven, four aspects are here picked out for convenience of examination, the connection with Modern Dance being explored primarily in relation to the first.

1. It is "without a preconceived or dictated style." The phrase is Ullmann's, inserted in the revised edition after the term *"free dance"* has been introduced for the first time (apart from its mention in the Preface). More positively, in Laban's words, "the whole range of the elements of movement is experienced and practised."

2. Modern educational dance is a participatory, not a spectatorial activity; it is not designed for an audience but is essentially for the benefit of the performer. "Experience" rather than an end product is thus what is chiefly valued:-

> It is not artistic perfection or the creation and performance of sensational dances which is aimed at, but the beneficial effort of the creative activity of dancing upon the personality of the pupil.

There are two considerations here, often referred to as the a) "expressive" and b)

---

* Except where stated to the contrary, all references in this essay are to the 1948 edition.

"impressive"; they will be dealt with separately, though they are held to be interdependent.

a) An explicitly stated aim is "to aid the creative expression of children." They "should invent their dances freely as a creative activity . . ." Modern educational dance is thus seen as "creative" and "expressive," the terms "creative dance" and "expressive movement" being frequently employed in contemporary educational discourse instead of, or interchangeably with, the original.

b) The psychological impact upon the individual is held to be of foremost importance:-

> Modern dance training has to be based on the knowledge of the stimulating power which movement exerts on the activities of the mind.

3. Complementing the stress on individual experience and personal expression, there is emphasis on group activity. The social as well as the psychological significance of dance is highly rated:-

> The immersing into a group dance gives the child the experience of the reciprocal adaptation of people to one another. Human relationships of a valuable kind can thus be promoted by group dancing.

4. Practice is founded on what Laban calls "principles of contemporary movement research," in particular, "modern work research":-

> The knowledge concerning human effort, and especially the efforts used by industrial man, is the basis of the dance tuition.

It is now proposed to examine each of these aspects in turn, and then to attempt, as it were, a salvaging operation. That is, those descriptions and explanations which appear inadequate as an account of an educational activity will be jettisoned, while those which do seem to be justified will be retained, though in some cases different grounds will be given, together with further reasons which it is contended have been omitted.

# C MODERN EDUCATIONAL DANCE

## 'FREE' ASPECTS

### 1. "Without a preconceived or dictated style"

The "free" nature of modern educational dance is the basis of its relationship with Modern Dance which, in fact, in both Europe and the U.S.A. was known as the "free" dance at various stages in its history. This aspect is to some extent bound up with the question of the movement principles on which practice is based, and will therefore be further investigated when these principles are discussed (section 4), and a different approach to the matter of "freedom" in respect of dance education suggested.

Meanwhile, since the term "free" has no application by itself, but always requires qualification in respect of former restraints and the choices subsequently open, it may be asked, "What is it—or the dancer and/or choreographer—free from? What is one free to do that was not previously possible (or fashionable, since artistic as well as social conventions may impose a sort of tyranny)?" Briefly, and fairly predictably, the answer would seem to be that it is liberation from "the fetters of a restricted number of traditional steps and gestures" (Laban, 1948) that is regarded as provided by Modern Dance, and freedom to create a greater variety of dance forms than before, using the whole range of movement available to the human body.

Although from a few minor references later in the text it would appear that the possibility is not ruled out altogether that traditional types of dance might have some part to play in the education of children, it is clear from the Introduction to *Modern Educational Dance* that Laban views both "the remnants of the historical art of dancing" and forms of social (or, as he calls them, "communal") dance as inadequate. The grounds on which they are so judged are at first, however, somewhat obscure, the discussion centring chiefly on the close connection held to exist "between the dance forms and the general behaviour, especially the working habits, of an epoch," which leads to the conclusion that "modern man has to build up his own art of movement." The implication is that dance, to be educational, must take account of "the conditions of life in our time" and of "the movements which contemporary man uses in his everyday life," and must, in addition, use "the flow of movement pervading all articulations of the body."

It is these two features which Laban claims distinguish "those dance forms which the Americans and, with them, other English-speaking countries, call 'Modern Dance'." This, however, may be questioned. American Modern Dance clearly originated in a desire to create new modes independent of existing European traditions and believed to be more appropriate and relevant to contemporary life, and in so doing drew on the manifold possibilities of the human body. But its history furnishes little evidence of a prime concern with twentieth-century "working habits" or "the efforts used by industrialised man" which Laban makes central to his account of dance as an educational activity. On the contrary, throughout its development in the U.S.A., there would seem always to have been a clear distinction between the study and practice of movement in the art form of dance, and in other, non-artistic activities—a lack of confusion which might well be the envy of dance educators in this country, where a misleadingly synoptic view of movement seems to have muddied channels of thought and procedure in dance (if not in physical education as well).

There is, nevertheless, no doubt that fundamental to Modern Dance, whenever and wherever it is found, is a concern with human movement, that in Sachs' (1937) words "the twentieth century has rediscovered the body," and that it is this which has rescued dance from impotence as a genuine art form and assures it of autonomy. The fact that movement is the "raw material" of dance, just as sound is the "substance" of music, may today seem so obvious as not to be worth stating, but it is none the less of prime importance, not least with regard to its educational implications.

As long as dance was tied to a plot or was strongly governed by music, so that it was to be judged mainly by dramatic or musical criteria (as was in fact the case at the beginning of the century, and still may be in the case of some kinds of dance), the substance of dance itself was only of secondary interest, subservient to considerations of other art forms. In addition, chiefly because of the dominating influence of the classical ballet of the period, attention was apt to be centred almost entirely on *positions* rather than on the nature of the *change* which occurs between them. But with the focussing of interest on the actual flow of movement it becomes possible to compose, and to assess the merit of what is composed, wholly in terms of kinetic ideas. Here it may be noted that although the term "flow" comes to have a very special significance (often with metaphysical connotations) in Laban's writings, it is a common, and indeed apt, expression in the literature of Modern Dance from Isadora Duncan onwards. Metaphors of growth and references to its "natural" unfolding or organic development in a dance often reflect this concern with the *progression of movement.*

For dance thus to become an independent art,* however, a comprehensive

---

* "Independent" here means logically distinct, i.e. having its own principles and canons of judgment—from which, of course, it in no way follows that a dance may not have a musical accompaniment, or be linked with the visual arts, poetry, and so on. To distinguish is not necessarily to separate.

system of analysing movement is essential. In the words of the 1963 edition of *Modern Educational Dance:*-

> Instead of studying each particular movement, the principle of moving must be understood and practised. This approach to the material of dancing involves a new conception of it, namely, of movement and its elements.

What is meant by "the principle of moving" will, of course, be all-important, but a fuller discussion of this is reserved until the final section of this essay, in conjunction with a survey of the particular contribution which, it will be maintained, some of Laban's ideas have to make in this connection. (This will in fact involve a reconstruction of the case for dance "without a preconceived or dictated style," since that presented by Laban gives rise to certain difficulties.)

The main point to be noted at present is that such a codification of movement must be appropriate to the activity of studying and practising it as an art form. A classification in anatomical, physiological, or kinesiological terms, for instance, while it might be of interest and even of some aid to the performer or dance teacher in relation to considerations of fitness, bodily functioning, and the programme of training, is of little use for the purposes of composition and for the understanding of a created dance form. Similarly, knowledge about movement as a manifestation of emotion is entirely irrelevant for dance which is simply "about" dance; and even when the subject matter does deal with human passions, the ordering of rhythms and patterns and the way in which particular parts or areas of the body are emphasised are to be assisted but little by an appeal to psychology.

Assuming for the time being, then, that a satisfactory analysis can be achieved, we might suppose that the educational values of dance approached from this angle were self-evident. Even if no arguments could be found to support the contention that children should engage primarily in dance as a practical activity, and it were held that they should learn only to appreciate dance as spectators, such an approach would still offer possibilities of gaining insight into a rich variety of dance forms. Just as some knowledge of the rudiments of music is indispensable to the appreciation of musical compositions, whether or not singing or playing or music-making is involved as well, so an understanding of the constituent elements of movement is basic to the ability to follow their arrangement and structuring in a dance.

But should the claim be allowed that practical performance in dance is educationally worthwhile, then the case is even stronger for the experience of a wide range of movement rather than the attempted mastery of one particular style or a limited selection of dance forms. For opportunities to take part are thus available to all, irrespective of individual differences in physique and temperament which may render conformity to certain modes entirely inappropriate, if not impossible, for some. Such a procedure is, of course, likely to go hand in hand with the development of a personal style through the *creating* as well as the *performing* of dances. (This will be referred to again in later sections.) What is pertinent to the question of dance "without a preconceived or dictated style" is that if it is argued that each individual should be enabled to use movement as an artistic medium, a rich and varied "vocabulary" on which to draw is clearly essential.

There is an obvious connection here too between the range of movement possibilities and the range of ideas, both kinetic and non-kinetic, with which dance can deal. Modern Dance, drawing as it does on the entire gamut of bodily movement, and denying that there is any gesture or posture that may not be legitimate or appropriate, is able to treat of a wide variety of subject matter. It is "free," that is, both in respect of form and content; it is confined neither to traditional techniques nor to what Laban calls "the dream world of fairies and princes." It is from this kind of standpoint that, for example, Valerie Preston-Dunlop (1963) makes the statement:-

> The aim of modern educational dance is not to learn one way of walking but to experience many ways, not one kind of posture but many, so that the body is a versatile instrument capable of being used at will and not an instrument which can do only a limited selection of movements.

Although this, as it stands, is misleading, since physical versatility could hardly be the *aim* of any educational activity, but only of instrumental value in achieving some further end, what this end is seems clear from her foregoing remarks. These imply that the need to be able to control the body in a variety of ways is viewed specifically in relation to dance as a creative and expressive activity. (Later she refers explicitly to the desirability of the dancer learning "to use his body as a true instrument of expression with a wide range.")

While this is implicit in much of what Laban has to say, there are in his account assumptions of a different kind which cloud the issue. These, as already explored in the previous essay, are chiefly embedded in his concept of "effort" and ideas revolving around this. In the light of his views about human nature and the body/mind relationship, and especially his notions of "effort balance" and "effort development," it is clear that he sees the practice of "the whole range of the elements of movement" as being of immediate and direct benefit to the individual, valuable *in* and *by* itself. This is all the more apparent when the elements to which he refers turn out to be the "effort" elements deriving from what he calls the "inner attitude" to the motion factors of weight, time, space and flow.

Laban's characterisation of dance as an educational activity is obscured too by his claims in respect of "effort training." Not only is it believed that all-round physical competence ensues from "the new technique," but it is assumed that such versatility is educationally valuable *per se*. Even if there were such a thing, however, as a general motor ability factor (which it seems clear that there is not), and even if bodily skilfulness of a general kind could be promoted by any one type of activity, it would not follow that to develop it would thereby be educational, any more than would be the case if it were to be shown that it resulted in good all-round physical development and functioning (no easy task, if only because of the difficulty of giving content to such a notion). Like physical fitness, this kind of versatility could at best be only of instrumental value, the activities in whose service such skill might be employed themselves requiring independent justification.

It becomes apparent that from a recognition of the overriding importance of movement to dance, it is an all too easy, but a somewhat dangerous step, to arrive at the conclusion that the study and practice of the "language" of dance (as distinct from the study and practice only of particular dance forms) leads to, or even necessarily involves, skilled performance and understanding of human movement in a great variety of contexts and manifestations. It might well be considered desirable that "the awakening of a broad outlook on human activities through the observation of the flow of movement used in them" (which Laban sees as one of the aims of modern educational dance) should be attempted in schools and colleges—that everyone should gain some insight into the significance of movement not only in the accomplishment of practical tasks as in work and sport, but also in personal interaction, i.e. through non-verbal communication, as well as in relation to personality. It may also be the case that such an awareness is assisted by experience of movement studied in connection with dance, that this can help people to be more observant of movement in everyday life. Students training to be teachers, for example, often claim that through modern educational dance they come to have a sharpened perception of the movement behaviour of both individuals and groups, as well as of rhythms and movement patterns within the animal world, in natural phenomena, in art, and so on.

This is all very gratifying to the teacher of dance, though it should not be altogether surprising. It would indeed be rather strange if, for instance, the student of painting were not more discriminating and critical in respect of colour, design, texture, and the like in the environment generally, and not only in pictures; or if the actor, as a result of his training, remained insensitive to such things as intonation, regional speech habits and everyday gesture. But such abilities and tendencies do not result automatically, and if they do not and it is thought desirable that they should, specific and appropriate means must be adopted to ensure the transfer.

One kind of understanding which may be gained incidentally during the study and practice of movement for dance purposes is, in fact, of a different genre from that involved in aesthetic activity and merits consideration on its own account, namely, knowledge of other people and of the self. The contribution that more thoroughly informed observation of human movement might make to this remains almost totally unexplored in education, but since personality and interpersonal communication are so closely connected with movement, there seems every reason why, as suggested in the first of these essays, such a study should be undertaken with older children and students in a systematic way. (See section 3, below.)

The significance of movement in relation to dance, however, is of educational importance in itself and, as will be argued later, the classification which Laban has formulated facilitates engagement in dance in a manner which meets the criteria for education set out above, without at the same time misappropriating an artistic activity for non-artistic ends.

# C MODERN EDUCATIONAL DANCE

Section

## 2a    ' EXPRESSIVE' ASPECTS

---

**"The beneficial effect upon the personality"**
**a) "Expressive" and "creative" aspects**

The assumption that modern educational dance is valuable because it is "expressive" and "creative" is one that is widespread, though usually completely unargued, throughout the literature of the subject (as, indeed, is apt to be true also of much written in connection with the arts in general). It seems often to be taken for granted that if children or students are engaged in "expressive" or "creative" activities they are inevitably being educated; and it is from such a presupposition that several writers canvass so-called "creative" dance or "expressive movement" and dismiss traditional dance forms as inadequate for educational purposes.

The concepts of "expression" and "creativity," however, bristle with difficulties, and there are particular problems in respect of their educational relevance. Some of those attaching to "creativity" have been referred to already in the first of these essays in connection with imagination (*see* pp.13-16 above) and will not be repeated here. To some extent they interlock with those belonging to "expression," though this has complexities of its own. It is therefore necessary to inquire into what can be meant by saying, for instance, that movement is expressive, that dance is a medium of expression (to which is often added "and of communication"), that "creative dance" provides opportunities for self-expression, and so on; and to consider how, if at all, learning to be "expressive" in this area is to be justified as educational.

In one sense—albeit a very general and not very illuminating sense—everything that we do is "expressive." Both what we do deliberately, either in word or deed, and what we do spontaneously and sometimes unconsciously, is a "sign" of our personality, a manifestation of our thoughts, feelings, desires, values, purposes, motives, and so forth. In this sense too all movement is expressive, but this does not take us very far in any attempt to establish its precise nature and function in dance. It also has to be recognised that movement is not capable of expressing just anything and everything. Although it is common practice among writers and teachers sharing Laban's views to speak of movement as expressive of *intentions*

*"Symptomatic" or "natural" expression*

71

and *attitudes* (as well as of moods, feelings, emotions, and other states of mind), such assertions are necessarily limited in their meaning. There is little doubt that there are many occasions when movement "speaks louder than words," when we think that we can infer more about a person's actual state of mind from his postures and gestures than from what he says, and when physical behaviour indicates more than speech either does or can. But it is conversely true that there is a great deal that movement alone *cannot* convey. It cannot, for example, express attitudes of the kind that are meant when we speak of someone's attitude to smoking, or to vivisection, apartheid, or polygamy; nor intentions, in the sense of what a man writing his name on a piece of paper intends by so doing (whether he is, for example, parting with money or prescribing medicine). Social prejudices, political allegiances, moral convictions, religious beliefs and the like are clearly not to be inferred from a person's movement as such.

As pointed out in the previous essay, bodily movement cannot be equated with *action,* and what we intend is often not at all clear from the movement itself. But it often reveals or betrays psychological states of a general nature. Thus, a person might write his signature carefully or carelessly, resolutely or timidly, and so on. (And it may be noted in passing that it would seem to be the rhythmic and spatial nuances of movement which, whether the observer is aware of this or not, are the chief basis of his interpretation.) In everyday life movement is frequently expressive in this sense, that is, it is *symptomatic* of inner states. But it is essential to distinguish this kind of expression from that involving deliberate formulation and articulation.

Perhaps an easy way to appreciate the difference is to compare someone weeping on one occasion with proffering an apology on another. In the former instance his tears *naturally* express (i.e. are a sign or symptom of) his sorrow—it is literally "squeezed" or "pressed" out; in the latter, his regret is *logically* expressed, (i.e. controlled, formulated expression). The difference is not simply one of the medium, movement in the one case, words in the other, though as Susanne Langer (1953) points out, "language is primarily symbolic and incidentally symptomatic," while with gesture the opposite is the case in ordinary life. Failure to distinguish this fundamental difference has been one of the most serious confusions besetting accounts of modern educational dance.

In particular, pointing to the connection between physical changes and emotional states can be misleading. Sometimes the latter are "expressed," that is, ooze out and overflow, without any willing on our part. We wince, shudder, go weak at the knees, and so on. Our bodily condition betrays or indicates our frame of mind. But these are events which we cannot help; we are not *agents* of such occurrences. Thus we are not engaged in action or activity at all, and such phenomena are wholly irrelevant to discussion of dance. On other occasions, such as when we bite our lip or shuffle our feet in embarrassment, the matter is somewhat different. Once again emotion is made manifest through physical changes, but though symptomatic they are not involuntary as in the case of shaking with anger or fear, jumping when startled, or fainting with relief; and though the individual may be unaware of what he is doing at the time, he can become so and to some degree control it. Such movement may include conventional expression of the state of mind in question, as in bowing the head in shame or lifting the eyebrows in surprise, and both in these and other cases is often learned from the particular culture pattern.

In all these instances movement which is symptomatic may be described as "expressive," but embarrassment, shame, surprise, etc. are not being logically expressed. Dewey (1934), much exercised about the notion of expression, declares in his *Art as Experience:*-

> Not all outgoing activity is of the nature of expression . . . . There is activity, but not, from the standpoint of the one acting, expression. An onlooker may say "What a magnificent expression of rage!" But the enraged being is only raging, quite a different matter from *expressing* rage. Or again, some spectator may say "How that man is expressing his own dominant character in what he is doing or saying." But the last thing the man in question is thinking of is to express his character; he is only giving way to a fit of passion.

This, of course, is to offer a stipulative definition of "express," but the importance of the distinction that Dewey is making is none the less crucial, and as he later says:-

> What is sometimes called an act of self-expression might better be termed one of self-exposure . . . . In itself, it is only a spewing forth.

Like Hospers (1946), who states that "a person may give vent to grief without expressing grief," he wants to reserve "express" for deliberate, controlled expression, and is rightly insisting that the "giving vent" variety has nothing to do with art.

Though this distinction is perhaps more generally appreciated now than formerly, it is nevertheless unfortunately the case that dance continues to be widely regarded as "a free discharge either of surplus energy or of emotional excitement," to use Langer's (1953) words. This, as she points out, is a naturalistic doctrine, and is subscribed to alike by "countless dancers" and "eminent theorists" (among whom she names Laban). And it is hardly disputable that early Modern Dance was strongly characterised by an interest in, if not actual display of, emotion.

*Art and expression*

The twentieth century "discovery" that dance consists essentially of movement was bound up to a considerable extent with the belief that what it is centrally concerned with is the affective life of the human being. Isadora Duncan (1927) described her dance as "an effort to express the truth of my Being in gesture and movement"; Mary Wigman (1966) refers to her art as "a living language which speaks of man"; "a dancer's world," says Martha Graham in her film of that name, "is the heart of man, with its joys and its hopes and its fears and its loves." Credos of this kind could be cited almost indefinitely. "Expressive dance" is, in fact, another of the many names by which Modern Dance has been known on both sides of the Atlantic, though perhaps being applied especially to that of Central European origin.

This is not, however, to say that dance which treats of human situations and passions and the "inner life" of man involves the performer in the *actual* states of mind concerned. On the contrary they are, to employ Langer's terms once again, "conceived" or "imagined"—no easy idea to grasp, as she herself remarks, especially for those accustomed to "the spontaneous emotion theory with which almost every modern book on the dance begins."

> It takes precision of thought not to confuse an imagined feeling, or a precisely conceived emotion that is formulated in a perceptible symbol, with a feeling or emotion actually experienced in response to real events. Indeed, the very notion of feelings and emotions not really felt, but only imagined, is strange to most people (Langer, 1953).

The view that art is centrally concerned with feeling, even though of the "imagined" kind is, nevertheless, itself to be challenged—indeed has been challenged, and Langer's own particular thesis that works are "forms of feeling" or "patterns of sentience," having a logical similarity with the structure of emotive life, viewed with scepticism (see, for example, Casey, 1966, Osborne, 1968, and Charlton, 1970). Expressionist theories of art, whether involving the idea that the artist's feelings are poured out in his work, or that feeling is evoked in the perceiver, or yet again that it, or something related to it, is somehow "embodied" in the work are, in fact, of comparatively recent origin within the whole history of art theory. In the West they gained ground only as late as the eighteenth century with the Romantic movement (see Osborne, 1968).

Though still very much in vogue in educational circles, the Romantic emphasis on emotional expression (using the term now in a broad and therefore rather loose sense) tends to be on the decline in modern art theory. It is, of course, recognised that art may, and often does, both symbolise and stimulate feeling, but it is no longer generally held that this is its only or chief purpose, or even a necessary characteristic. As Findlay (1967) puts it:-

> A complex set of numerical or quantitative relations, a contrast of qualities, a strange affinity of seeming disparates, the remarkable logic of some ingenious theory, the atmosphere of a historical period, etc. etc., may be what is well expressed in a piece of poetry or music, and not any specific emotions connected with the latter.

But however "abstract" a dance composition may be, however mask-like the face, it seems that dance is always to some extent *connected with* feeling. A "space harmony" composition may have nothing to do with ideas about the human condition as such in the way that, say, Kurt Jooss' "The Green Table" or Martha Graham's "Night Journey" have. Yet the very fact that movement of the human body, indeed, of the human being, is the vehicle of meaning makes it difficult, if not impossible, for our experience of movement in everyday life to be completely divorced from it in dance. Reid (1970) has noted this peculiarity :-

> Dance is never pure in the sense of being *only* a pattern of sheer movement in space . . . . The medium of gesture, expressive human movement, is intrinsically meaningful, though it is not possible to say exactly what it means once it is part of dance.

This becomes apparent if we consider, for example, a lifting of the body as compared with one of lowering it. Such a movement may, of course, be performed in an almost infinite variety of ways, each with differing nuances of expression, but although in dance it becomes "transformed" in being structured within a particular context, it nevertheless retains something of the everyday significance which it has within our own culture. This may fall within quite a wide range of human experience, associated perhaps with pride, or elation, hope, visionariness, aspiration, or a whole host of other less easily nameable states of mind. But what would seem to be true is that it *precludes* the range belonging to the contrast of sinking, falling, or pressing downward, associated with the experience of despair, defeat, determination, or security. At least it operates negatively, if not positively.

Yet the force of such associations may be reduced to a minimum, and, as maintained in the previous section, dance has never been more capable than now, with a comprehensive analysis of movement available, of being simply "about" dance. In contrast to the trend in the first part of the century, Modern Dance in the theatre during more recent years has been less exclusively concerned with the expression of human feeling and has endeavoured to fulfil its potential as a kinetic image having no meaning beyond itself. In education, on the other hand, "creative dance" or "expressive movement" is still apt to be thought of as primarily a matter of expressing feeling. There are, further, two other aspects of the expression theory of art that are allied to this idea, and that make an appeal to many educationists, but which are liable to distort aims and procedures in education. One is that the aim of aesthetic activity is to effect the *relief* of feeling; the other that through it the child or student expresses *himself.*

Because of the close connection already discussed between bodily change and the manifestation of feeling, dance (with, to some extent, drama) is of all the arts most likely to continue to be thought of as providing an outlet for pent-up emotions and a release of tension. But in Laban's *Modern Educational Dance* there

*Expression and relief of feeling*

is nowhere any reference to the cathartic aspect of movement. Whatever errors in this respect may have been perpetrated by other authors and teachers, and whatever has been done or said in schools and colleges about the purging or relieving of emotions through dance (and in the early days particularly this *was* sometimes said and attempted in practice, thus understandably bringing the subject into disrepute), this does not owe its origins to anything that Laban states in this book; though, as will later be shown, he is ambivalent about the connection between dance and emotion.

The one mention of the removal of "frustrations," which might be thought to imply such a notion, occurs within the context of an argument that "dancing relieves the feeling of discomfort produced by the repression of general bodily stirrings during isolated joint actions." This quite clearly refers, however, to the kind of "frustration" alleged by Laban to spring from the loss of general physical mobility, and of "the enjoyment of the balance of efforts" which dance, since it "gives an aesthetic pleasure, like the colour scheme in a picture or the harmony of sounds in music," is claimed to provide. As will be evident from the previous essay, this is all bound up with his ideas of "effort balance" and "effort harmony," and is rather different from the popular view of emotional frustration and its relief through art.

Furthermore, although Laban's account of modern educational dance revolves around his theories of "effort," and stress is continually laid on the importance of the "inner attitude," he does not say merely that "whatever is danced should be executed with full inner participation," but adds "and clearness of form." Unfortunately, the force of this extremely important point is reduced by his next remark that "the creative stimulus and the awareness of the enlivening and freeing influence of dance movement are all that is desirable." This is precisely what is *not* sufficient in any educational, as distinct say, from recreative or possibly therapeutic activity. But attention to the formal properties of a particular medium (accent, shape, phrasing, etc. in the case of movement), and to their organisation in an art product make for the controlling of the "feeling" content it may have, and for preventing any tendency on the part of the artist or the perceiver to indulge in an excess of sentiment.

In addition, Laban is explicit that "it is erroneous to take dance as the language of emotionality only," and asserts that "it is rather a language of action" (though what exactly this means is not altogether easy to decide). This is stated in connection with the last of the sixteen basic movement themes which are put forward as the foundation of a comprehensive scheme of dance training, this last being in fact the only one of the sixteen to deal specifically with "the expressive qualities or moods of movement." Throughout this exposition attention is directed exclusively to the "moods" accompanying various combinations of movement elements, and in particular to what he calls "action moods" (the inherent expression, that is, of sequences of "basic effort actions").

Laban might seem here to be implying that dance "moods" are *sui generis* and, though sometimes related to reality, are somewhat different from the *emotional* experiences of everyday life. They are *movement* "moods," to be known and understood only through this medium. This is not unfamiliar talk. Many artists and aestheticians maintain that what is variously referred to as the "meaning" or "expression" or "import" of a work of art is specific to the formulated whole in question, and does not otherwise exist. And we may recall Wollheim's (1971) claim, mentioned in the previous essay, that in a work of art a mental state or condition becomes known by the artist which he could recognise in no other way. (See p.53 above.) What Laban might be thought to be saying at this point is that the structures of rhythmic/dynamic elements of movement as ordered and related in a dance are not adequately characterised (though they are often vaguely described) as, for example, "happy," "aggressive," or "dejected."

> In calling rhythms wild or soft, frightening or appeasing, we do not give more than a very general idea of the mood they evoke (Laban, 1958a).

Nor, it may be added, are they to be equated with the expression of emotions, which are essentially directed towards "objects"—we are afraid *of* things, angry *with* people, ashamed *that* . . . etc. (See next section.)

On several occasions Laban is emphatic on this point. In "Dance as a Discipline," a paper published posthumously in 1959, he says:-

> Very many dancers are not emotional at all, even if they awaken emotions in the spectator . . . . The ideas expressed by dance belong to a stratum of the human spirit which should not be labelled as emotion.

And in an excerpt from an unfinished article entitled "Meaning" (also published in 1959), he affirms:-

> It must be realised that it is of little help to say that such and such a movement is the expression of such and such feeling, emotion, passion, or other inner activity of the dancer.

Later, speaking of national dance, he seems to recognise quite clearly that dance is not a piece of everyday, commonplace behaviour, serving some biological or psychological function, but rather a kind of "as-if" activity, symbolising, abstracting and expressing in the logical sense:-

> Selection and filtering of movement took place which divested formerly real actions of all their concrete usefulness until a true symbolic action resulted. The final form has acquired a definite and new meaning. . . . *

---

* This is remarkably akin to a passage in Bullough (1912) discussed by Langer (1942). Much of this paper on "Meaning" would seem, indeed, to be influenced by Langer's chapter on "Significance in Music."

Yet from time to time it does sound as though Laban confounds the articulation of *imagined* or *conceived* feeling in dance with the expression of *actual* affective states, and in common with many others he is apt to be led by the verbal connection between "motion" and "emotion" to suppose that dance must involve genuine feeling. This might be partly due to the fact that, as also often happens in ordinary speech, he uses the word "emotion" rather indiscriminately, so that it comes to apply not only to affective states of all kinds,* but also to the "inner" life in general. In *Choreutics* (1966) "action moods," which are described as "of a purely expressive nature, originating from within the person and containing mental and emotional qualities," are not characterised as unique to dance, as might appear from what is said in *Modern Educational Dance,* but are alleged to belong "both to life and to the stage." And in *Mastery of Movement on the Stage* (1950) there is a constant tension between Laban's idea that "efforts" and mental states are *of the same kind* in work, play, prayer, dance, and all other human activities, and his insight into the fact that the organising and structuring of rhythms and shapes in art makes for an essential difference. He says, for instance:-

> It is the arrangement of the efforts of everyday life into logical yet revealing sequences and rhythms which gives a theatrical performance its special character.

It is not clear, however, by what criteria this "arrangement" is governed, and how we are to distinguish what counts as "logical" from what does not. What Laban persistently seems to overlook is that what constitutes "logic" in dance is of a wholly different order from that distinguishing other forms of movement activity. Though sharing the common feature of bodily movement, these various activities are not susceptible to the same kinds of judgment: the domain of the aesthetic is distinct from (though not necessarily unrelated to) the ethical, the scientific, the religious, the mathematical, and so on. These are all examples of what Wittgenstein (1953) calls "language games" or, as Oakeshott (1962a) describes them, "voices" in the "conversation of mankind," each having a specific character and manner of speaking of its own (cf. also Reid, 1961, Phenix, 1964, and Hirst, 1965).

Langer (1953) draws attention to the same confusion of actual and imagined feeling in Laban's German writings, though she maintains that he "understands none the less that dance begins in a *conception* of feeling," and quotes him as saying in an early work "conception is everything." This is one of the chief things which renders his whole account of "educational" dance so problematical. It is presented both as an artistic, and yet a non-artistic, "ordinary-life" activity, and claims are made for its educational value on the ground of the experience it is held to provide of actual moods and human situations. At the end of the section on

---

*cf. section 2b, below.

theme sixteen in *Modern Educational Dance* referred to above, for instance, he is plainly talking of moods that occur in everyday life, not *dance* moods, as appeared to be the case earlier; and a justification of dance as a curriculum activity seems to rest on the basis of its usefulness as an exercise in discovering and controlling (though not releasing) *real* emotions:-

> Children of the later senior age-groups have an urge to explore their own and other people's moods. Much help can be given to them when dance tuition in these critical years is adapted to the aim of clearing up the sources of irritating situations and habits and making them thus less important and less dangerous.

This, as it stands, is implausible, though few would deny the truth and importance of the first statement. What Laban is in fact speaking of here is not an *aesthetic* mode of experience, but an aspect of *personal and interpersonal understanding*. As already suggested, (see also section 3 below), the latter might well be increased *indirectly* as a result of participation in dance, but this will not be because the "moods" of the individuals concerned are indistinguishable from those met with in situations of day-to-day living. There is, however, the germ of another argument in this reference to the exploring of moods through dance which is pertinent to the complex issue of affective education, such as Bantock (1967) puts forward in *Education, Culture and the Emotions*. That is, experience of art (which of course extends to learning to *appreciate* as well as *make* artefacts) may be a prime means of developing an understanding of *new* sorts of feeling, and of "refining" existing ones through the presentation of more highly differentiated varieties of those which are yet crude or indeterminate. An important feature of at least some kinds of art is that it involves varieties and shades of affective experience of which we are less likely, or less easily able, to be aware in ordinary living, perhaps because they are not readily identifiable or precisely nameable.

Laban, however, does not consider "educational" dance from this point of view. It is always presented as an activity aiming at the attainment of *actual* states of mind, and the *inducing*, or perhaps the "exercising," of these through movement seems to be accorded rather more importance than any *expressing* of feeling or thought (though often Laban does resort to this way of speaking). We therefore reach the point of overlap with the "impressive" aspect of the subject, and further examination of the nature of "action moods" will be continued in part b) of this section. Meanwhile, it may be remarked that the "moods" of "floating," "gliding," "thrusting," and so on, of which we hear in the discussion of theme sixteen, do not seem of the same order as those which people usually have in mind when they refer to the discharging or relieving of feeling through movement and other "expressive" activities.

As far as cathartic effects of dance are concerned, if Laban (or anyone else for that matter) *were* counselling the inclusion of dance in the curriculum primarily, or even secondarily, for such reasons, such a recommendation would be entirely misguided, not to say thoroughly dangerous. Not only is this to subscribe to an instrumental theory of art, i.e. valuing it for the results believed to ensue from it, rather than just for what is in it, thus imposing criteria which are not *artistic* criteria; but it is also to confuse the task of the teacher with that of the therapist. To suggest that children (or students) *in general* need release from emotional strain is to suppose that the majority are already suffering from such stresses. And even if it were true that many *were* beset by problems of this kind, and if (which is extremely doubtful) a teacher knew how to cope with ten, or even one, let alone forty "sufferers" placed in his (more likely her) charge, for the purpose of "expressing" their bottled-up emotional energies through movement, he would be compelled to abdicate from his role as educator and strive to fulfil one for which he is neither equipped nor intended.

As Bantock (1967) has insisted, the nature of the transaction between teacher and pupil is essentially a pedagogic one, and to provide opportunities for "creative" work in schools and colleges in order to encourage release from tension, thus treating art as relaxation, is to fail to recognise human creativity as involving a "perpetually renewed, demonic, immensely joyous struggle with intractable material and media, through which man achieves some measure of control and transcendency over the internal and external worlds. . . ." And when that "material" (perhaps the most intractable of all!) is the human being himself,* how much more lamentable and hazardous is it to indulge any flabby desire for emotional gratification by wallowing in sentiment, or pseudo-sentiment, rather than engaging in a "joyous struggle." Such a "toughening" process, which is an inescapable and vital aspect of all creative work might, in any case, prove to be *incidentally* effective in the case of emotional disorders.

**Expression and communication**  Before consideration is given to the matter of self-expression, brief mention may be made of another thread within certain theories of art which connects with this, and which is also of an instrumental character—namely, that expression involves communication. Usually this is bound up with the view of art as a language of feeling, and as serving the purpose of edifying and educating the spectator or listener by evoking emotions and other states of mind which are believed to have inspired the artist. Obviously this is not what is meant by references to communication in Laban's account of modern educational dance, since it is conceived of from the point of view of the performer, and is held to be for his benefit alone and not for that of any onlooker. The query then arises as to whom communication is between, and what the nature of this communication is. The implied answer to the latter is highly problematical, as once again there seems to be

---

* One is reminded here of Martha Graham's reference to dance in her film, "A Dancer's World," as "the handling of the material of the self."

a confusion between dance expression and that of ordinary life. The answer to the former would appear to be "Between the dancers themselves." This point is thus tied up with that feature of modern educational dance which lays stress on group experience and social considerations; further inquiry into the question of communication will consequently be undertaken in the section devoted to this subject (see pp. 109-110 below).

Creative activities in schools are often, perhaps even chiefly, regarded as Self-expression instrumental in a way somewhat different from the view just discussed, though not unrelated to the idea of art as the expression of feeling. That is, they are seen as a means of permitting, and indeed encouraging, the expression of the individual's *personality.* It is the child *himself* who, it is claimed, is "expressed." Even where cathartic notions of art are not countenanced and no undue stress laid on emotion, it is common to meet with talk of the overriding importance of giving scope for expression, through various media, of the individual's own ideas and experience. And in the 1940s and 1950s especially, modern educational dance was welcomed by many "progressive" educationists precisely because it was seen as capable of fulfilling this "need" in the field of movement.

In this respect "creative" dance is, of course, in direct line with Modern Dance in general, which in turn was part of the Romantic tradition. The key concepts of the latter—individualism, creative imagination, originality, expression, communication, sentiment, etc. (admirably discussed by Osborne, 1968), were precisely those espoused by the proponents of the "new" dance of the early twentieth century. "In the so-called 'Modern Dance'," Langer (1953) observes, ". . . dance is a self-portrait of the artist"; and whatever recent trends have been, it was originally distinguished chiefly by a desire "to externalise personal authentic experience," in Martin's (1933) well-known phrase.

It is thus associated with the dancer himself composing his own dances, not only (and in some cases, not at all) performing those of others, and so "expressive" dance becomes linked, if not identified, with "creative" dance. Such compositions are therefore seen as having deep personal significance, both because the individual is encouraged to retain and develop his own "natural" style of moving, and because of the opportunities that "free" dance makes available to him to express his own point of view, and to dance (Graham's words again) "the deep matters of the heart."

Such ideals, coinciding as they do with the aims and procedures of the "child-centred" movement in education in this country, have been widely canvassed in connection with modern educational dance, though there is little explicit emphasis on this aspect of "expression" in Laban's writings. Most children, it is true, lack that kind of life-experience which prompts utterance of the profoundest kind in poetry, dance, drama, painting and so on, and they could hardly be expected to participate profitably in dance conceived of primarily as an activity concerned with "his existence as a human being played upon by life, bursting with opinions and compulsions to express them" (Humphrey, quoted in Cohen, 1966). But many educationists argue that it is important for even young children to learn to give form to ideas and feelings which *are* within their grasp and of significance to them, and that dance "without a preconceived or dictated style" makes this possible in a way which, say, classical ballet or any other specific dance form could not. (And as pointed out in the first of these essays, a child's movement inventions *might* be a useful indication to the teacher of the way in which that individual thinks and feels about a particular situation, though clearly this cannot become the *aim* of the enterprise.)

Probably few people would quarrel with the idea that part of art education, in its broadest sense, does consist in the articulation of life-experience, but it can hardly be claimed that this is the whole account. For children or students to be confined to attempts to express their own viewpoint in the arts is as restrictive as for them to be presented always with examples, studies, patterns and styles on which to model their efforts. The "literature" of the various art forms—pictures, sculptures, musical compositions, poems, novels, plays *and* dances, is indeed an important means by which we come to have something to "say" (cf. pp.19-21 above). It is as much a reality and an aspect of concrete experience as a visit to the zoo or the law court, the exhibits on the nature table or experiments in the laboratory, a holiday by the sea or an archeological "dig." If we extend what Oakeshott (1962b) says about learning our native language ("what we say springs always from our manner of speaking") to the learning of the "languages" of art, it is evident that *what* can be expressed is partly, and perhaps largely, determined not only by what others have "said," but also by *how* they have "said" it. And though there is as yet a serious shortage of artefacts of good quality in dance suitable for educational purposes, it remains highly desirable that children and students are introduced to the compositions of others. As mentioned in the first essay (A) above, one has only to consider the impoverished nature of their understanding of music and poetry, for instance, if their experience of these were limited to their own inventions or those of their fellows; but the enrichment of their whole concept of dance through participation in, and also watching of, dances and dance-studies which they themselves have not composed tends to be somewhat neglected.

Furthermore, without some knowledge and skill in the particular discipline involved, they can hardly be expected to make their experience articulate—even if it makes sense to suggest that there *are* first precise ideas and feelings which *then* find expression (cf. p.20 above). Osborne (1968), discussing the view that they are apprehended only in and through the expressing of them writes:-

It is by the expression of his feeling in art forms, this theory maintains, that an artist comes to terms with it, gives it contour and shape, actualises it for apprehension. It is by being clarified through the formative impulse of art that the formless and elusive feeling tone and mood which accompany all our perceptions . . . acquire in the case of the artist both structure and precision. The obsessive character of the artist's impulse to express his feeling in artistic form derives less, it is claimed, from the desire to communicate his feeling to other men than from the need to apprehend it himself. By formulating it in art he as it were digests it, makes the inarticulate articulate and gains relief from the unassimilable pressure of the unknown and formless.

If this applies to children and people in general as well as to the artist, it has important implications for educational practice. Yet it unfortunately often seems to be assumed that because we all have a body, and because this is the channel of spontaneous, natural expression, a ready source of dance is at hand, and that one has only to provide some stimulus to switch on and tap this supply. (It is even sometimes supposed from this line of reasoning that students in colleges of education can teach without any specific experience or training themselves!) It might as well be argued that since we all have richly "expressive" vocal capacities, ranging from murmurs and groans to shrieks and cries, we are automatically able to sing—and, more than this, to compose songs. In any case, as Reid (1957) says:-

"Self-expression" gets the emphasis all wrong, and is apt to flatter egotism where there should be humility and outward-looking joy. Stress upon "expressing oneself" suggests that "oneself" is too interesting. It tends to introversion, selfconsciousness, sometimes unhealthy preciousness.

And of course there is no guarantee whatsoever that the results of self-expression are either of aesthetic merit or in any other way *educationally* valuable in the strict sense. This is by no means to deny, however, that they may have advantages of a different kind, and that (in spite of the inevitable vagueness of "health" and "wholeness") there is an important truth in Reid's further remark about young children that "it is for their health and wholeness that they dance and jump and shout and scribble and make mud pies." This "ceaseless activity of experimental doing" may well be, and probably is, a *precondition* (and in *some* cases an aspect) of formal, in the sense of institutionalised, education. And as Reid further points out, "expressing themselves" in these spontaneous, unguided ways and so working off, or working out, their fantasies is probably good both for "normal" and "abnormal" children. But while all this may be necessary for educational progress, it is not sufficient. However fresh and sincere their attempts may be, unless children and students are helped to produce works of increasingly good quality by public standards, their *aesthetic understanding* will be limited,

As already noted, everything that we do is "expressive" of our personality (the criminal laying and carrying out his plans, be he master crook or petty thief, may fairly be said to be engaged in an act of self-expression); and recognition of the fact that something of the artist is inevitably reflected in his works is of long standing. But the idea that self-expression is the main function of art, or a justification of it,

84

is of relatively recent origin. Osborne (1968) asserts:-

> To say that an artist expresses himself by his art, trite as it now seems, would
> have been an incomprehensible or a rather stupid irrelevance to classical
> antiquity and the Middle Ages or the Renaissance.

It is yet another feature of the Romantic attitude from which art education seems
to find it hard to escape.

"Movement expression"
There is scarcely any reference, however, in *Modern Educational Dance* to the expression of the child's *life-experience* or to the question of subject matter in the sense of ideas external to movement itself. The stress throughout is on the sufficiency of *movement* material, and when Laban states that "children should invent their dances freely as a creative activity," it seems clear from the context that what is considered as constituting such dances are extended sequences involving combinations of various movement themes. These sequences are thus comparable to paintings which emerge from experiments with colour, line, texture and so on, rather than of the kind having a mainly representational or "feeling" character. (It is indeed explicitly recommended that "dance plays with a story should be used sparingly.") When Laban *appears* to be speaking the same language as those who urge the provision of opportunities for the personal expression of the child, he is in fact almost always referring to *movement* expression and the development of kinetic ideas rather than any other sort. Mastery of the whole range of movement elements, as noted in the previous section, is never discussed by him in relation to the desirability of children becoming equipped to deal with a variety of subject matter in dance, but exclusively from the point of view of the benefit to them of the *experience* of movement itself.

Nevertheless, while it has been suggested that the underlying rationale of Laban's advocacy of "effort exercise" is of dubious validity, it has also been maintained that his recommendations in respect of "effort training" are wholly pertinent if this is interpreted as implying the progressive mastery of the dynamic and rhythmic aspects of movement (see previous essay). This is both a fundamental part of dance education and, in its very "concreteness," able to be adapted to the capacities and understanding of children through various stages of development. The rhythmical elements of movement, their contrasts and combinations, their increase and decrease within a phrase, their development to reach climaxes, pauses and so on, are of intrinsic importance in dance. This is not, however, the case in drama and mime where they always serve some further idea. Starting with non-kinetic ideas and "expressing" them, leads to a stress on representational movement, often with a corresponding lack of concern with its formal properties. This of course is not to undervalue the important role which movement has in drama education, but its function and significance in the two arts, even allowing for hybrid forms such as dance-drama, are different, and the difference lies in the extent to which the structure of the rhythmic and spatial patterns of movement is in itself the meaning.

It is indeed a curious fact (and something of a disaster for dance in education) that, in spite of Laban's actual suggestions in respect of practical procedures, which involve exactly that kind of classification and systematisation of formal elements necessary for dance, the activity itself is widely associated in the popular mind with mimetic and expressionist views of art. This is not to pronounce a formalist theory as *the* "true" one, nor indeed that any one art theory is sufficient for dance or any other art form (cf. Weitz, 1962). Many dances are to be judged, and in fact succeed, by criteria of all three kinds (i.e. mimetic or representational, expressionist *and* formalist); and, as is clear from his references to Noverre and Duncan in the introductory chapter to *Modern Educational Dance,* as well as what is known of his own productions in the theatre before he came to this country, Laban was no pure formalist. But in education emphasis on the "expressive" aspect of dance often seems to lead to a confusion of aims and of the standpoint from which children's work and progress are to be judged; it tends to a one-sided and limiting view, and to hamper the extension of their horizons in this area.

The main issues in this complex and often confusing subject of expression in **Summary** movement now call for summary:-

1. Like "creative," "expressive" is an ambiguous term, its varying uses taking on different meanings according to its context and application.
2. The connection between physiological changes and bodily movement on the one hand, and natural expression of feeling and emotion on the other, is largely irrelevant and misleading when the nature of dance as an aesthetic activity is considered, and arguments advanced for its place in education.
3. *Symptomatic* and *symbolic* expression must be distinguished. Even folk dances (and this applies too to a good deal of contemporary social dance), which may be assumed to have sprung from "the spontaneous overflow of powerful feelings," are essentially *forms* which are symbols, rather than symptoms, of the original mood or occasion which promoted them; and though they may involve "imagined" or "conceived" feeling which corresponds in some measure to the original, they are none the less different from the initial phenomenon which was an outcome of *actual* feeling.
4. Dance does not *have* to be "about" feeling at all either in the theatre or in education, although there is probably an ineliminable element of this kind in all dance. Movement elements which are ordered and structured as particular rhythmic and/or shape configurations in dance are meaningful in their own right. Much dance, however, will probably continue to be inspired by the events and experiences of human existence, ranging from, for example, the "Birthday Dance" of an Infant class, to the sophisticated reflections of the college student

or professional choreographer.

5. Dance education, which includes learning to appreciate as well as perform and compose artefacts, thus has an important contribution to make to the affective life of the individual, both by providing new experience of the "standard" emotions, where these are presented with fresh insight and vividness in mature dance works, and by opening up to him shades and varieties of "moods" not otherwise accessible. But it is *not* concerned with the purging and releasing of undesirable emotions and tensions, which in any case is not the business of the educator. This does not rule out, however, the possibility that participation either as a performer or a spectator might be incidentally of assistance in this respect through the disciplining nature of the activity.

6. To be educative dance does not have to be creative in the sense of being composed by the performer, or expressive in the sense of reflecting his personal life-experience. Dancing expressively extends to dancing the compositions of others, and a variety of experience of both kinds would seem desirable, though many factors such as the ability of the children or students concerned, and the availability of suitable artefacts, will obviously affect the balance of the total programme.

# C MODERN EDUCATIONAL DANCE

Section

## 2b    'IMPRESSIVE' ASPECTS

---

**"The beneficial effect upon the personality"**
**b) "Impressive" aspects**

To many people talk of the "impressive" power of movement and dance often suggests that reference is being made to the experience of the *spectator,* that what is implied is that the *audience* is moved, or in some way affected by what they see. This of course is a perfectly understandable and reasonable reaction, particularly in view of the widespread acceptance of expression theories of art mentioned in previous pages—namely, the assumption that through the art object the perceiver is enabled to share with the artist the feelings believed to have inspired his work.

But, as in the case of communication, it is not any concern with the impact on the onlooker which characterises writings about modern educational dance (although this is not held to be unimportant in the case of dance which *is* intended for an audience, and is indeed valued). By contrast, it is the effect of bodily movement on the moving individual himself that is constantly emphasised; its "impressive" character is, as it were, the other side of the "expressive" coin. Just as movement *reveals* a person's "inner life," so (thus runs the argument) it also leaves its impress upon his mental state. It *affects* as well as *reflects.* Laban (1948) states:-

> We do not sufficiently realise the important effect action has on the mental state of the mover. Movement can inspire accompanying moods, which are felt more or less strongly according to the degree of effort involved.

This is basic to his account of "educational" dance as a participatory rather than a spectatorial activity, and of key importance to the twin claims that "it is not artistic perfection . . . which is aimed at, but the beneficial effect of the creative activity of dancing upon the personality of the pupil," and that it is "of educational value to base dance tuition upon the principles of contemporary movement research." He (1948) confidently declares:-

87

The impact of movement on the mind has been studied, and it has been found that movement consists of elements which create actions reflecting the inner efforts underlying them.

Here then is pure dualism, and we are back, as might indeed be expected, with "effort" and "knowledge" purported to have been established in industry about the reciprocal influences of mind and body. Obviously, as already indicated in the inquiry into "Effort" (Part I), this relationship is an issue of enormous complexity and perennial debate, and here it is possible only to touch on some of the most salient problems to which such claims give rise and on some of their educational implications.

First, it might be observed that traditional philosophical accounts of the body/mind relationship seem to pay hardly any attention at all to the question of the effect of the physical on the mental from the point of view of bodily movement (though the reasons for this become clearer when the matter is further investigated). Attention centres chiefly on physical events such as receiving a blow, or the impinging of light-rays on the retina, resulting in mental events such as (respectively) pain, and visual awareness; or on the effects of such things as drugs on states of mind. Perception and sensation seem to have commanded more interest in this connection than emotion and other affective states.

Yet it seems obvious both from experience of everyday life, as well as fiom knowledge of social and ritual dance, that movement can influence our mental condition. We may, for example, brace ourselves physically (literally "take a grip" on ourselves) in times of crisis, or conversely try to relax—and this not always simply to control or hide the manifestation of feeling, but in the belief that by so doing we can, for instance, strengthen our resolve, calm our excitement, or snap out of an apathetic mood. But are we not *evidencing* the desired state of mind in the very act of bracing ourselves, relaxing, speeding up, slowing down, and so on? Laban's own thesis is that to produce movement of a particular kind (say, a "basic effort action"), requires already being in the corresponding frame of mind. The whole notion of "effort" as "an inner impulse originating movement" entails this, and he further states:-

What happens psychologically is that the moving person after receiving the suggestion to perform such functional action [i.e. one of the eight "effort actions"] * puts himself into the indicated state of mind, so that the movement comes out with a certain degree of spontaneity and freedom . . . (Laban, 1952).

Then again, something of a "chicken/egg" situation seems apparent in his

-------------------------------------------------

* My insertion.

suggestion that changes in mental states result from habitual movements which are performed unthinkingly (and perhaps unknowingly), as well as those which are produced in response to a teacher's promptings in a situation of an essentially physically active kind. Returning to *Modern Educational Dance* we read:-

> Small movements of the face and hands, or of isolated parts of the body, are as expressive of the child's mental state, and have as much effect on his mind, as larger movements . . .

What is "expressive" thus becomes "impressive," and presumably vice versa. What we are is manifest in what we do; what we do makes us and confirms what we are. The point here seems to be that repeated movement intensifies its character and reinforces the accompanying mood. Hence also, perhaps, Laban's mention of the *degree* of "effort."

In discussions of the ("symptomatically") expressive character of movement it is often apparent that he recognises that a particular type of bodily activity may indicate a great variety of mental states and that no exact one-to-one correspondence is to be found. He observes, for example, that among primitive peoples "hopping from one leg to the other has different meanings," and lists joy, surprise, anger, fear, "and many other states of excitement" as possible sources of such expression (Laban, 1961). But in respect of *impression* he is apt to talk as if there is an unvarying correlation between particular movement patterns and inner experience. "A specific movement," he says, "may have each time a similar impact on the child's mental and bodily attitude" (Laban, 1948). This however is to ignore the fact that the "same" movement may, and frequently does, take on significance of widely different kinds according to the context, and will therefore vary in its effect on the performer.

If someone performs a series of "thrusts" or "punches" in exchanging blows in a fight, for example, he is not engaged in the same *action* as when he "punches" or "thrusts" in a dance sequence. Though we may point to similar features of rhythm and shape within the movement content of the two cases, the vastly different intentions and aims of the agent, and how he views what he is doing, must produce contrasting psychological effects. Surely stabbing a piece of meat with a knife does not bring about the same sort of impact on the mind of the doer as if he were to stab a human being, nor is either comparable in its effect with that of practising "thrusting" gestures in a dance training session, in spite of the similarity of the "effort" structure of all three acts, or of any other movement features they might share. "The absolute congruity of man's working movements and his expressive movements," which Laban (1950) finds "a staggering revelation" is only an external congruity.

*How* a movement is performed gives no information by itself of *what* a person is doing and this (and more particularly what he conceives of himself as doing), cannot be of secondary significance in relation to his mental state, but must be of

*Bodily movement and human action*

signal importance. As mentioned in the previous chapter, an *action* can never adequately be characterised by reference to bodily movement alone. To take Wittgenstein's famous example of raising an arm (or of a longer sequence of movement, should it be objected that a single gesture is relatively uninformative): however much detail about such an occurrence might be provided by movement experts, whether on the basis of Laban's classification, or from an anatomical, physiological, or any similar point of view, this is irrelevant to determining the nature of the *action* or *activity*. Such an event does not carry its meaning on its face; it is intelligible only within a social form of life, in which it might serve as a secret signal, an expression of boredom, a request to be allowed to speak, or a host of other things. It is therefore unthinkable that the function which movement has in differing situations does not affect the performer, or that simply by virtue of consisting of the same movement components different acts can have an identical influence on his mental state.

**Movement and emotion** But perhaps it is to be assumed that Laban is thinking in terms of the psychological effects of movement as practised in the context of dance (though in *Effort* this is obviously not so, since here he is concerned, among other things, with the moods produced by repetition of working actions). Even if the concern is with movement "for itself," however, there are certain kinds of experience which it is logically impossible to attain by bodily movement alone. It may therefore be asked what sorts of mental states are, or could be, capable of being generated by this means.

The question is one belonging to philosophy as much as to psychology, and in particular to philosophy of mind. Analyses of emotion concepts (see, for instance, Peters, 1961, Kenny, 1963, and Bedford, 1965) show that, contrary to the popular view (often subscribed to by advocates of the arts in education), emotion is not something which exists without thought. Reason and passion are not always, as traditionally characterised, diametrically opposed; there is, on the contrary, an intimate connection between the two. It is, for example, impossible to experience hope without *perceiving* something in a favourable light; to suffer guilt or remorse without *believing* that we have done wrong; to be proud or envious without *appraising* some "object" (whether an achievement, a thing or a person, etc.) as desirable. In other words, having an emotion depends on our *interpreting* and *evaluating* situations and occurrences. "X feels bitter about the way he has been treated" carries as an indispensable part of its meaning: "X *judges* that he was treated badly," "X *believes* that he ought not to have been so treated." Cognition and emotion are thus bound together,* and the old idea of independently

---

* It is because of this connection that a young child is incapable of a whole range of emotions such as compassion, shame, indignation, contempt, gratitude, contrition, etc., which presuppose notions of time, cause and effect, and means-ends connections; as well as an understanding of a host of complex social relationships, institutions, and systems of judgments of a moral, legal, and aesthetic kind.

functioning faculties (deriving from a pictorial model of the mind as an entity, or an instrument, or a place, consisting of various parts), is now thoroughly outmoded. It is only in exceptional circumstances that apparently unaccountable emotions such as "nameless dread," "blind rages" or "free-floating anxiety" occur, and these very adjectives, Peters (1961) points out, indicate the need for special explanation.

As Kenny (1963), underlining the distinction between emotions and sensations, puts it:-

> It is possible to be in pain without knowing what is hurting one. It is not possible to be delighted without knowing what is delighting one. It is not in general possible to ascribe a piece of behaviour or a sensation to a particular emotional state without also . . . ascribing an object to the emotion.

Having an emotion is certainly not simply (and some writers even insist, not at all), a case of experiencing a determinate, recognisable, and essentially private *feeling.* Traditional accounts along these lines fall down as soon as we realise that if this were so and emotions were known only by introspection, the meaning of emotion words could never be learned. We should have no way of checking that the experience we label, for instance, "grief" is what others also call by that name.* An emotional state is identified typically by reference to the circumstances to which it is related; it is not to be *equated* with a bodily state, or movement as such, even though there is, of course, a close relation between the two.

If, for instance, a teacher notices that a child is very pale, trembling, and perspiring, she cannot tell merely from the physical symptoms whether he is terrified or sickening for some disease. Nor is any amount of detailed observation of the "effort" content or spatial structure of his movement, either on its own or in conjunction with the noting of physiological reactions, ever sufficient to determine the matter. It is only within the wider context of his *behaviour* (verbal and/or non-verbal) that this can be settled. It is not bodily movement alone which provides evidence for the conclusion "He is afraid," but typical *fear-behaviour* such as seeking to avoid danger, or some answer to the question "What's the matter?" (which itself illustrates the point), such as: "Tommy's got a mouse in his desk!"

In Wittgenstein's (1953) words:-

> No matter how we describe a piece of behaviour, it will only be *emotional* behaviour if it occurs in the appropriate circumstances.

Without some "target," as Kenny (1963) terms it, for let us say, fear, there is rarely fear-behaviour, and no *bodily* condition can be designated a state of fear.

---

* For an easily readable account of how mental terms are learned, see Shaffer (1968) on "pain."

To influence a person's emotions, therefore, it is necessary to influence his *beliefs*, the way in which he *thinks* about the situation in question; and it might well be that, even though different emotions were evoked on different occasions, similar *movement* manifestations would occur. It therefore follows that no genuine emotion could be induced *simply* by moving in a specific manner. Thus Laban's (1948) emphatic assertion:-

> It cannot be stressed too strongly that the movements the child experiences have a marked reaction on his mind, so that varying emotions can be induced through his actions . . .

is manifestly implausible if "actions" is taken to refer (as he often intends) to bodily movement as such. This is not a hypothesis to be checked against empirical evidence; it is a logical impossibility, since whatever mental state might be brought about by movement alone would not be what we call emotion. Nothing that falls within this category could conceivably occur other than in a context in which responses to actual events and situations involving beliefs and evaluations were involved.

Even in the case of dancing such as that performed by primitive tribes before going off to an actual hunt or battle, it may be recognised that it is the reality of the situation which is responsible for the onset of the genuine emotion. As soon as such practices become divorced from their real-life context, become truly ritualised and thus acquire *intrinsic* value, we leave the realm of raw feeling and enter the field of art. Here there is a *detachment* (albeit of a kind peculiar to art and not immediately easy to comprehend),* from emotional and practical involvement in what Coleridge calls "the world of selfish solicitude and anxious interest." As Osborne (1963) puts it, "the mood-implications of the object [i.e. the art work] † are enjoyed without the vicissitudes of the mood-experience."

If a primitive dancer were to break away from the dancing mob and rush off from the dancing place in pursuit of the quarry, unable to contain his excitement any longer, this might be understandable.** If, by contrast, a stage dancer were to behave in such a way he would himself probably be pursued and treated as suffering from a delusion! Similarly, we do not expect children or students in a dance class to sit down, run away, or burst into tears, on account of the "emotions" induced. As teachers we should rightly be surprised and concerned if such emotion-behaviour occurred, and would probably seek to provide reassurance by saying, for example,

---

* See pages 139-140 below
† My insertion.

** Even in these circumstances such an event might prove unlikely. Apart from the tradition which gives little scope for individualism, in dance which is already bordering on ritual and is not, in Sachs' term, mere "prancing," spontaneous impulse is in general subordinated to what approaches artistic discipline.

"We're only imagining"—just as in comparable circumstances where reality and non-reality are confused, the reminder is given that "It's only a story," or "It's only a game!"

It is nevertheless not impossible that something *akin* to an emotional state (a sort of synthetic or pseudo-emotion) might be aroused by bodily movement as such, because of the fact that we learn to identify emotions in the first place in the context of physical behaviour, which includes their "symptomatic" expression. We thus come to associate their manifestation with certain features of movement. But circumstances would have to be such that the emotion would not be inappropriate. If, for instance, a workman is apt to be discontented in his job, impatient with the management, or anxious in general, work requiring rapid, jerky action might well render him more discontented, impatient or anxious than a job demanding mainly slow, smooth exertions. *

It could, on the other hand, be argued that movement characteristic of the expression of a particular emotion (in the "giving vent" sense) might be expected to *provide relief* rather than *intensify* it. Either way, the result would not be due to some mysterious "inner" process set in motion by the physical exertions, as in the case of the flow of blood to some part of the body to which a hot compress is applied. *No causal mechanism is at work here.* Rather, the person has become acquainted with certain manifestations of, for example, frustration, and is put in mind—"re-minded," as it were, of what it is like to display frustration. Perhaps this is why, on some occasions we speak, for instance, of something making us *feel* angry (i.e. as we feel when we actually are angry), while on others we say that it *makes* us angry (i.e. genuine emotion).

We have also to realise that there are no exactly specifiable manifestations of every emotion. As Osborne (1968) points out:-

> Darwin himself admitted that the varieties of expression are not adequate to discriminate the varieties of emotion known to popular wisdom and enshrined in common knowledge . . . . Anger and indignation 'differ from rage only in degree, and there is no marked distinction in their characteristic signs' . . . . Extreme contempt 'hardly differs from disgust'.

And in Laban's classification, though it is of a wholly different kind, not dealing with movements such as frowning or dilating the nostrils, there is no demonstration of a one-to-one correspondence between a specific emotion and specific structures of movement elements. Moreover, many kinds of expression of feeling are governed by social convention and cultural tradition. Consequently, how far and in what way movement can be "impressive" varies to some extent according to the particular culture pattern. What is learned in this respect, however, and more

---

* Such an example is necessarily oversimplified; much would depend on the nature of the recovery phase within the total process—which is precisely where Laban's ideas of rhythmic balance, or "effort harmony," have application.

especially what is "picked up," is the significance not only of *a* particular movement (e.g. widening the eyes, which to the Westerner conveys surprise, but to the Chinese anger), but also of the more subtle and spatial nuances within that movement. We thus discern *mild* or *intense* surprise, *gradually increasing* or *shocked* amazement, and so on; and through Laban's differentiation of "effort elements" we are able to establish precisely what it is in the movement that we notice and that leads to our conclusion. In the absence of cross-cultural studies along these lines, however, it is impossible to know how far interpretations of observations involving more complex rhythmic aspects of movement are universal.

But the "action moods," "effort drives" and "effort attitudes" which he categorises are not, as he constantly emphasises, adequately described in verbal terms. (This is not to say that there could not be such words, but they would have to be invented specially for the purpose in order to avoid the usual connotations of already existing expressions.) Certainly the states of mind correlated with these various "effort" compounds are not to be equated with those which are directed towards a "target" and distinguished by characteristic emotion-behaviour. They are nearer to those of an "objectless" or "unattached" variety such as in everyday language are perhaps more appropriately termed "moods."

**Movement and mood**    If we return for a moment to the case of a workman's mental state being affected by the nature of the movement he has to perform, it might be generally agreed that it would be less accurate in such circumstances to speak of sorrow, pride, awe, jealousy, shame, hatred, hope, and such like, than of more general states such as irritability, depression, excitement or agitation. These might become attached, as it were, to a particular "object"—for example, to his job prospects or working conditions, and so develop into a full-blooded, concrete emotion. But otherwise, they remain, in Osborne's (1963) words, "like a floating charge on the furniture of the mind" and, rather than being focussed on a "target," are "here and everywhere, like an atmosphere or an odour, or a diffused toning of colour, lending a special flavour . . . to anything that comes into (my) mind." And the best we can do by way of verbal description seems to be to use terms such as "elated," "serene," "restless," "sombre," "boisterous," "contemplative," "vivacious," "dreamy," and so on.

Now these are the kinds of mood-words which are also used to describe dances, pictures, pieces of music, and the like. And although one of the most knotty problems in aesthetics is this attribution of qualities of feeling to works of art* (since it seems to amount to the absurd proposal that affective states are discernible in non-sentient objects), in dance the difficulty is perhaps rather less acute inasmuch as, in contrast to other art forms, its material is *not* inanimate, but exists

*See, for example, Hepburn (1961), Morris-Jones (1962), Osborne (1963), Wollheim (1968), Reid (1969) and Charlton (1970).

in the human being himself. Without becoming embroiled in the complex but intriguing question of what exactly a dance is (the choreographic score? the performance? the conception behind the performance? etc.) we can appreciate that for its presentation living beings (not simply pieces of matter or sound waves) are required, whose movement it is far from absurd to suggest expresses *moods*.

This therefore brings us nearer to the issue of the sorts of states of mind with which the dance teacher is concerned. Clearly, to try to induce those we designate *emotions* is out of the question. Even if this were possible through movement alone (which, as we have seen, it is not), and even in the case of pseudo-emotions, it would be a highly debatable procedure, and could moreover be morally repugnant, to seek through the medium of dance to bring unsuspecting individuals into mental states of this kind—especially impressionable young people in a situation which they may very likely not have entered voluntarily. As Bantock (1967) stresses, because of its connection with conduct "the incidence of emotion comes to be subject to ethical judgment."

Nor does it seem likely that Laban is actually putting forward any such proposal. As noted in the previous sub-section, he tends to use the term "emotion" in no very exact way, and the claim that "movement can inspire accompanying moods" is much less strong than that in respect of emotions. Specific combinations of movement elements would seem to be more closely related to moods of the "objectless" kind, unfocussed on any particular event or situation of ordinary life, than to emotional states. And when, as in dance, concentration is on these elements (and, in the case of "effort" elements, on what in *Mastery of Movement,* 1960, is called the "sensation" aspect), the performer is likely to become more acutely aware of, to be put in touch with, so to speak, the state of mind required to produce the sequences involved. Because of the precise structuring of movement elements in dance, such "moods" become more sharply defined and more clearly recognisable than in everyday living, although, as suggested in Indian aesthetic theory (see Osborne, 1968), the moods of art seem to be more specific to the work itself, and more universalised and generalised than those outside art.*

What Laban would seem to have in mind when he speaks of the beneficial effect of movement, and especially of dance, on the mental state of the performer are what he variously describes as "contentment," "joy," "a unified experience of space and time," and "a feeling of unity" which, as he says, makes the dancing person "happy and free" (Laban, 1961). The nature of these states of mind will be examined more closely later, but meanwhile it becomes evident why *experience* in modern educational dance is prized more highly than *achievement* ("achievement" meaning not simply an end-product in terms of a highly polished composition or a performance, but what is publicly observable as opposed to what is inner and

---

* cf. also Wollheim's (1971) thesis that "if someone can recognise in something that he's made a reflection of an inner state, it is often the case that he would not have been aware of this state except through the object or objects that he makes." (See p.53 above).

private). This, however, raises certain difficulties.

We might well go along with Laban in holding that "sensational dances," "exemplary productions" and " striking works of art" should not be the chief concern in education, if by these adjectives is meant elaborate and pretentious stage shows. But it is such descriptive terms applying to artefacts which invite objection, not the assumption that there should *be* artefacts. For how else are we to characterise, let alone estimate, the "beneficial effect of the creative activity of dancing upon the personality of the pupil"? How can we otherwise tell *what* his experience is? There is nothing that can be stated about the thinking and feeling of others (in the absence of their own testimony), without reference to their observed behaviour. This is a matter of vital concern to the teacher, because unless the experience of the children or students is externalised through some performance or product, how can he know how far, if at all, he is succeeding in his aim(s), or judge and assist progress?

Two suggestions seem to be put forward, if somewhat indirectly. The first is that successful participation in dance is shown by signs of absorption, elation, ecstasy, and other allegedly desirable states of mind. But one can be absorbed by the trivial, ecstatic yet sentimental, and elated by what is crude and shoddy. As educators, we have cause all too often to find that this is the case—a situation which is exacerbated by a lack of readiness on the part of some teachers to distinguish between the standard of achievement and the effort a pupil makes (which might be considerable and certainly deserving of commendation, but nevertheless result in work of poor quality). To fail to help children and students themselves to appreciate this distinction, and to lead them to suppose that praise is being given for the work as judged by objective criteria, rather than for the energy and enthusiasm which may be displayed in its production, is to withold from them the very means by which they may improve, and become able realistically to appraise both their own attempts and those of others. Far from constituting kindness, this amounts to deception, and is particularly reprehensible with older children, who may receive a rude shock when eventually they realise, as sooner or later they must, that the merit of their attainments, as judged impartially, is not what they had been led to suppose.

Moreover in dance, as in any other pursuit, states of absorbed concentration, delight in the activity itself and intense involvement are no guarantee that what is being done is worthwhile; important though they may be, they are not enough. There is also the further point that it is highly debatable whether states of ecstasy and of absorption *into* or *by,* as distinct from *with* an activity are to be welcomed in education. Sachs' (1937) claim that "every dance is and gives ecstasy" applies much less to dance as art than to dance of the recreative, magico-religious type, in which states of mind ranging from mild euphoria on the one hand, to rapturous oblivion on the other, are deliberately sought. Though there may well be an ecstatic element within dance as an art form, it is always part of the *conception* of the work itself, and not simply (if at all) a psychological condition of the performers. Nor is it the *point* of the activity that they should attain such a condition. This would be to confuse an artistic undertaking with an attempt to use dance as a stimulant, a palliative, or some kind of self-hypnosis. Even if sense is to be made of movement as "an independent power creating states of mind frequently stronger than man's will" (Laban, 1948), to try to employ it in this way has no place in education. Indeed it is to fail to accord others due respect as persons* to involve them in some process in which they, so to speak, lose touch with, or stand apart† from themselves and reach a point where the movement takes over, so that they do not know what is happening to them as opposed to understanding what they are doing, and acting as responsible agents (i.e. being conscious in the paradigm sense). It would therefore be morally indefensible as an educational procedure, much less an aim. Being "taken out of oneself" to a moderate degree might have some place in a therapeutic or a recreational situation, but it can hardly rank as the legitimate business of an educator.

There is of course little danger that even the most fervent teacher of dance would set out to send a class into a trance-like state! Ecstasy among students and older children is more likely to take the form of sentimental self-indulgence and emotional wallowing in movement. In *Modern Educational Dance* Laban does not talk explicitly in terms of ecstasy, and as will later be argued his recommendations for practice, as exemplified in the material of the sixteen movement themes, provide an admirable basis for the pursuit of dance as an artistic activity, rather than a recipe for intoxication. But allusions to "immersion into the flow of movement" do suggest that dance is consistently thought of as a means of attaining a "higher" state of consciousness. This is especially so when they are read in conjunction with similar references in his other writings, which reflect something of a preoccupation with dance as ecstatic experience, a dedication to that mystical flow whereby man passes, in Sachs' words (1937), "into the void, into that expanse where the self mingles with the infinite . . . where willing and thinking are blotted out." As Curl (1966, 1967a, 1967b, 1968a, 1968b, 1969) has shown, the "philosophic foundations" of Laban's "space harmony" theories are traceable to Pythagorean doctrines of ecstasy, harmony and cosmic unity. (This does not necessarily invalidate, however, the usefulness of his systematisation of spatial relationships for the purposes of dance training and dance invention; see section 4 below.)

In "Dance in General" (originally given as a lecture at Dartington Hall in 1939,

---

*On "respect for persons" see, for example, Peters, (1966) and Downie & Telfer, (1969).
†Webster's dictionary gives for ecstasy; "1. State of being beside oneself; state of being beyond reason and self-control, as when obsessed by a powerful emotion. 2. A state of overmastering feelings, esp. joy, rapture. 3. A mystic, prophetic, or poetic trance . . . in its strictest sense, a trancelike state . . ."

but not published until 1961), Laban clearly wants to suggest that there is a type of dance activity which is different from both the recreational/social and the art form of dance. He proposes that "the matter of dance" may be divided into three "parts" (from the point of view, it would appear, of the different purposes which dance may fulfil). These are "the art of dancing," "dance education," and "the science of dance." It is not at all clear exactly what distinguishes each of these. In "the art of dancing" he includes "festivity dances" which, however, he recognises "serve solely as enjoyment and recreation," while "the science of dance" sounds very like what in *Modern Educational Dance* he calls "the technique of moving." But "dance education" seems to be connected with, or to be perhaps a development of, what he has earlier referred to as "natural dancing," and to be conceived of as some special and rather superior sort of play which produces "contentment and joy" and "a feeling of unity." Similarly in *Mastery of Movement on the Stage* Laban states:-

> It children and adults dance—that is, perform certain sequences of effort-combinations for their own pleasure—no audience is necessary . . . . Dancing—or at least that which today we call dancing—is, however, different from play, but it is not in itself a stage art . . . Dance is a stylised play . . . . (Laban, 1950).

The development of personality    The other kind of "evidence" that would seem to be proposed as a basis for judging how far a performer is benefiting from participation in dance is the increase in his "effort" range. Development of personality, we are told, "depends on an increase in the range of effort-capacity" (Laban, 1950). But as maintained in the previous essay, this is inadequate without reference to the ends towards which such development of "efforts" is directed, and to their ordering and structuring in relation to the standards internal to the activity in question. We are therefore inevitably brought back to a consideration of the quality of the individual's achievement.

A major source of difficulty in a great deal of modern educational dance literature is that the development of personality is seen as an enterprise somehow different from that of the development of knowledge and understanding. But as Oakeshott (1967) has argued, this is a false antithesis. The seeming dilemma which, as he says, has haunted education for so long, embodied in questions such as, "Is learning to be understood as acquiring knowledge or is it to be regarded as the development of the personality of the learner?" and "Is teaching concerned with initiating the pupil into an inheritance of human achievement, or is it enabling the pupil to make the most or the best of himself?" is not a dilemma at all. A personality does not grow, a mind is not formed, independently of the differentiated modes of thought and awareness which are specifiable and testable in public terms; and to suppose that these can in some way be bypassed and yet the individual become enriched as a person is to misconceive of the nature of mind and of human development.

The idea that there are abilities or mental qualities *of a general kind* which can be promoted through any one form of activity or discipline is mistaken. It is therefore vacuous to talk of dance, or for that matter, any other single pursuit, fostering creative imagination and powers of communication, developing insight and sensibility, sharpening perception and judgment, and the like, on a wide front. Exactly what is meant by any of these can be recognised only in respect of particular types of accomplishment, and their manifestation will vary from one domain to another. As Hirst (1965), criticising severely such assumptions in the Report of the Harvard Committee, "General Education in a Free Society," makes clear, the use of broad terms like these conflates quite disparate achievements. What counts as "effective thinking," for example, in aesthetics is not appropriate in mathematics; what "communication" in the sciences shares with poetic "communication" is minimal.

It is not merely that Laban makes claims such as that "the cultivation of artistic taste and discrimination in general cannot be furthered better or more simply than by the art of movement" (Laban, 1948). He is also apt to speak in imprecise, global terms such as the enhancement of "life powers," the establishment of "inner and outer balance," the strengthening of "human functions," the increase of "life forces," the achievement of a "unified and balanced process of living," and, perhaps most repeatedly, "the integration of feeling and thinking." Since no explicit positive content is given to ideas such as these, and in the absence of any clear specification of the means by which such psychological processes or conditions may be recognised, phrases of this kind have no meaningful application.

Only when a particular metaphysical view of the human being and his universe is **Dance and** understood can the implications of Laban's insistence that dance as an *educational* **"unity"** activity is for the doer alone be fully appreciated. His paper "The Importance of Dancing" (published posthumously, 1959c), clearly reveals his belief in a pre-established harmony of existence and function in all living creatures, and in "natural laws" which "extend their influence far beyond the realm of purely physical and biological functions"; together with a conception of dance as an "inner urge to move in harmony with the source of life and actually with the whole of the universe." This "inner urge" (also referred to in *Modern Educational Dance),* the purpose of which is to "maintain the connecting flow between the manifestations of life and their natural lawfulness," is seen as characteristic of animals, primitive people and children. But "civilised" man, with his intellect (or "mental knowledge," or sometimes simply, "mind"), all too often fails to obey this "mysterious compulsion to perform seemingly purposeless movements," and so loses his "first innocence." This must therefore be regained by the "impregnation" of the whole being with "the beneficial rhythms and wonderful trace-forms" which in the unspoiled creature "emerge from the depths of its urge to play." As Curl

(1969) points out:-

> Laban's whole philosophy revolves around the desire to promote an order and harmony in man's movement, which he believes to be in a state of disorder, and as such, detrimental to individual and social well-being.

Hence, Curl maintains (with reason, it would seem), Laban's frequent mention in his teaching of "chaos."

"Educational" dance is thus a form of recreation, albeit "re-creation" in a highly specialised, but problematic sense. Laban (1959c) declares:-

> To 're-create' is to create something afresh, something which has been weakened . . . it is . . . a re-establishment of lost and weakened relations and connections with the source of life.

If, however, we do not share such a metaphysic (or even we do, but realise that the attainment of harmony of this sort would be essentially a private experience and not publicly checkable), the notion of dance being purely for the promotion of a sense of well-being in the performer has to be abandoned. By the same token drug-taking and sexual pleasures might have to be considered educative.

And when we look further into what can be meant by phrases such as "the fusion of feeling and thinking," "integration of body and mind," "the blending of action, thought, and will," "a feeling of unity," and so on, which regularly occur in Laban's writings about the effect of harmonious movement on the psyche, what seems to emerge is the conception of a form of consciousness (if indeed it can be thought to be such) in which thinking, willing, etc. as they are usually understood, even in a weak sense, could hardly be said to be going on at all. Such activities seem to be suspended, transcended perhaps—or, as Sachs has it, "blotted out." In one of the most telling passages in which he describes "the feeling that accompanies the state of ecstasy" in dance, Laban (1961) speaks of "that kind of extreme concentration which we call unity of body and mind," but during which the dancing person "is nearer to a natural and less conscious life." He goes on:-

> He is in a state of mind comparable to the one we sometimes experience, for instance, in our sleep, when we seem aware of nothing but a simple feeling of existence.

Far from enhancing keener intellectual discrimination and heightening affective experience, the result therefore sounds more like a state of dimmed perception, and undifferentiated awareness, which is of course quite the reverse of the development of mind which is a vital concern of education.

Yet Laban is not unaware of the dangers of uncontrolled ecstasy, and when he wants to refer to that kind which is, by contrast, disciplined but active and wakeful, it is significant that he almost invariably turns by way of comment and illustration to discussion of the *art* of dance. Here he recognises quite clearly that the "moments of inner fulfilment" which he (1957) claims "all real art brings" only occasionally become ecstatic, "but not as a rule, and certainly not as a terminal human aim." In his talk too of "unity" and "flow," what it is sometimes not impossible to conjecture that he has in mind is the *artistic unity* of the dance work itself. There are even indications (especially in "Meaning," 1959b), that he is groping obscurely towards that kind of conception, familiar in modern aesthetics, of the unity of the art object and of apprehension of it by a direct act of non-conceptual synoptic perception (*see* Osborne, 1968). His use of the term "confluence" is particularly interesting in this respect. But all too often his references to "unity" are part of a confused amalgam of notions ranging from the idea of unity within nature and of the human being's awareness of *his* unity *with* nature, to that of the unity of conscious and unconscious function, and "unity" in the sense of a general feeling of elation and well-being.

Had Laban pursued the idea at which he occasionally seems to hint (see pp. 76-77 above) that "moods of movement" are *sui generis* and become *publicly* as well as privately known only when they are made articulate in a structured form, his claim for dance to be of educational significance would have been indisputable. As it is, with his presuppositions about an ideal order of the universe and the child's inborn urge to move in harmony with it, the grounds which he advances are all too likely to be dismissed as impossibly metaphysical and unworthy of serious debate.

To summarise this discussion so far:-

1. While it is common experience that bodily movement can influence the mental state of the performer, the connection is not of a direct *causal* kind; its "impressive" power is dependent on its "expressive" character.
2. Since all movement occurs within a context, that context, and not simply the manner of moving, will affect the doer. However similar the movement content of two different *actions*, differences in intention and aim on the part of the agent will have correspondingly different psychological implications.
3. Emotions, which have essentially a cognitive core, cannot be induced solely by the performance of particular movement patterns. In any case, for an educator to try to use movement in this way in the name of dance, even if such a procedure could be shown to be morally defensible, is to misunderstand the symbolic nature of the activity.
4. Because, however, we learn to identify mental states through their physical manifestation, they come to be associated with certain features of movement, and a person may be "re-minded" of a particular state of mind through moving in a particular way. There nevertheless appears to be no straightforward one-to-one correlation between specific movement patterns and the states of mind we know by name. The connections we learn to make are, moreover, subject to cultural variation.

5. In dance, as a result of the associations we have learned in everyday life, certain structures of movement tend to carry certain mood suggestions. But each particular structure of movement elements which is a dance may be regarded as manifesting a unique state of mind achieved by the artist.

6. Claims for the educational value of dance cannot be in terms of private, inner experience, for which there is no independent check, but must rest on achievements to which public standards apply.

7. The development of personality cannot be secured in an overall, general way by any one type of activity, but involves differentiated awareness and understanding. Dance is *one* mode of understanding within the total fabric of experience.

**Children and "presentation"** There are, of course, different reasons why some educationists hold that dance is for the doer only, and one consideration which may very likely have led to an acceptance of the view that an "end-product" in modern educational dance is relatively unimportant is that of the unfortunate side-effects that sometimes follow the presentation of finished items by children (especially young children) to an audience—as may also happen in the case of drama. Many teachers of these subjects know that, without considerable experience, children are prone either to suffer from sheer paralysis on such occasions, or to indulge in embarassing displays of cleverness or sentimentality, and there may often be a concern with superficial aspects at the expense of sincerity and artistic involvement.

But it does not follow that what is subject to public standards has to be shown to an audience other than that of the teacher and other members of the class. *The making and performing of artefacts and their appraisal in accordance with objective criteria does not entail that they are formally presented.* Assuming that the teacher is himself knowledgeable both about dance as an art form (which necessarily involves being able to engage in critical discussion and evaluation), *and* about what can reasonably be expected of children at various stages in the light of their experience and ability, it is perfectly possible for some understanding of dance as an art to be achieved without pupils engaging in large-scale productions.

Nevertheless, that performances for others to watch should never be included in the dance programme, particularly at secondary school level, is seriously to be questioned. Clearly, careful preparation and training for such presentations are essential, just as is true in the case of poetry reading, or the performance of musical items or a play for an audience. But the new skills in projection and communication which are required provide a further dimension of experience and understanding, the value of which it is difficult to deny once children reach an appropriate standard. It seems to be a fact of human nature that in the performing arts at least, an extra "something" is produced in effort and enthusiasm when there is a specific end in view, particularly one involving public appraisal, and in schools and colleges much is to be gained from groups of dancers and individuals presenting items of a good standard on both formal and informal occasions.

In the case of primary school children, too, who sing songs and play instruments and act dramatic scenes "for" others, and whose paintings, models and other achievements are regularly displayed, it seems a pity that the sharing of dances should not similarly be encouraged from time to time. And while with young children dance is obviously nearer to the kind performed for sheer pleasure, an educator must none the less be clear about the actual nature of the activity. Considerations of progression and of how experience is to be widened are always to be determined by criteria belonging to an aesthetic discipline. An understanding of dance as an art form begins when concern is not simply with delight in bodily movement, but with a formulated whole, a structured "something" (be it only one or two rhythmically ordered phrases), so that the relationship and coherence of the constituent parts become of increasing interest and importance.

In addition, the viewing of dance performances in which the major concern is with the dance itself, and not whatever is taken to be the psychological experiences of the dancers, is a most important part of dance education (and one which Laban, with his not inconsiderable interest in children's theatre, certainly recognised). The logical outcome of an adherence to the doctrine of "dance for the doer," at the expense of concern for standards of achievement, is that dance is relegated to the category of optional leisure-time pursuits and regarded as having no claim to a place in a curriculum already overcrowded by subjects amenable to public appraisal.

Finally, it is worth noting a different way in which the "impressive" nature of movement and dance may be viewed. This is most explicit in Preston-Dunlop (1963), where "impression" is used always in connection with the development of a personal style through experience of "harmonious and universal dance forms" (more accurately, as she calls them elsewhere, "movement forms"). In her discussion of the undesirability of the teacher creating dances and studies for children which are "strongly flavoured with his own personal style of movement," the value of knowledge of Laban's space-forms (scales, rings, etc.) is argued:-

*"Impression" and personal style*

> It is during the practice of studies that most impression is made on the style of the individuals in the class, and it is the teacher's responsibility to see that this impression is a harmonious one. . . .

That movement can be "impressive" in the sense that it leaves, as it were, an imprint on the performer's manner of moving can hardly be disputed. The dancer versed in Graham technique or classical ballet, the show-jumper trained in German as distinct from Scandinavian style, the skier brought up on old-time Austrian rather than Norwegian methods, is clearly recognisable by his physical perform-ance in the particular activity in question—indeed he may find considerable difficulty in breaking away from that style should he wish to do so. The point here, however, is almost the exact opposite. Not only is it maintained that "impression" is necessary for "expression." ("Before articulate movement expression can be achieved," Preston-Dunlop asserts, "the movement factors of shape, quality and rhythm must have made an impression on the individual . . .") But experience of harmonious forms of movement, it is claimed, enable the child or student to develop his *own* style of dance, and unless the aim of performing pre-choreographed dances and studies is to become acquainted with these forms, "the educational value of the work is hard to find."

What exactly is to be made of the notion of "harmonious and universal forms" in the field of movement is, however, left unexamined, but since this is bound up with the whole question of Laban's "principles of movement," further consideration of this point is deferred until the last section of this essay. All that needs to be noted at this juncture is the close relationship between "impression" and "expression" which Preston-Dunlop's references illustrate, and the assumption that the former, as a teaching method, is justified in the interests of the latter. She in fact states in the Preface that "this is a basic principle of the teaching of Modern Dance and an essential one if the work is to be called Educational. "By implication, therefore, it is not of educational value to be introduced to particular styles of dance.

---

**Social aspects of modern educational dance..**

The question of whether modern educational dance is to be regarded as an aesthetic mode of experience, or something else, is brought into prominence as much by reference to its social aspects as any other.

The opportunities which it affords for responding and adapting to others spontaneously in movement situations, for group co-operation and for shared creative endeavour, have always commanded special interest among, and have become highly valued by, educators. Many indeed claim that it is quite unique in this respect. It also seems true to say that it has widespread appeal precisely on this score for many children and students. But what is the nature of the relationship between those who take part, and what are the specific aims of the teacher in promoting such relationships?

Laban, it will be recalled, states (1948) that

> The immersing into a group dance gives the child the experience of the reciprocal adaptation of people to one another.

The metaphor is of some significance. It is, of course, natural to connect the flow of movement with the flow of water, and the opening passage of the last chapter of *Modern Educational Dance* where this reference occurs is almost a paean in praise of flow!

> The flow of movements fills all our functions and actions: it discharges us from detrimental inner tensions; it is a means of communication between people . . .

And, as is often the case in Laban's writings, not far away from talk of "flow" are ideas of unity and ecstasy and the universal harmony (see section 2b, above). He speaks of "that dreamy part of our being which has been called the soul," and asserts that

One who during his school days has not learned to appreciate the immersion into the universal flow of movement does not know that such a thing as a universal flow exists.

With his belief in laws of harmony governing the whole of creation, it is not surprising that what he sees as the prime means of establishing (or re-establishing) connections with this order (see "The Importance of Dancing," 1959) should be thought to make also for interpersonal, as well as personal, harmony. Since the individual personality can be "harmonised" through the ordering of his movement in accordance with these laws, it follows that through group dance which is similarly regulated, harmonious relationships with his fellow-men can also be achieved. It might therefore seem likely that the experience Laban has in mind in speaking of "total immersion into the flow of movement" in company with others, is of a mainly ecstatic type, the dancing individual "infecting" other dancers with the spirit of his own dancing, and in turn being "infected" by theirs.

This at any rate seems to have characterised much of the "choric dancing" or "movement choir" type of activity which enjoyed so much popularity among lay people in Central Europe in the 1920s and early 1930s—chiefly, on Laban's own evidence (see Laban, 1955), on account of the "communal elation" thus generated. He also (1961) states:-

> Man does not content himself only with motions and emotions which he has, so to speak, inflicted upon himself. He has also the desire to act upon some-body or something, to influence and to attract other beings and to drag them into the whirl of reciprocal action and reaction.

If, however, such "immersion" implies being dragged into a whirl of mass motion and emotion, and a certain loss of a sense of individuality within the larger unit of the whole, then this is nearer to what is involved in dance as a social-festive, magic or religious activity, than to dance as art, and is hardly relevant to (and might in some cases even be considered antipathetic to) education. On the other hand, at least in his later years, Laban was strong in his condemnation of "emotionality" in dance, over-indulgence in "play-like enjoyment," and "sheer dreaming" (see Laban, 1958b), and in his paper "The Work of the Art of Movement Studio" he (1954) states:-

> In the art of movement there is an artistic element which can be found in the use of expressiveness in all the forms of training. The expression is, however, not rapturous or dreamily vacant. On the contrary, the trainees *are made aware of what they are doing,* without spoiling hereby their spontaneity. (My italics).

But as in the case of "expression," there is nearly always in the literature of

modern educational dance a confusion between the relationships and communication of ordinary life and of dance, of the actual and the 'virtual'. It is perhaps
nevertheless understandable, in view of Laban's conception of "educational"
dance as an activity for the benefit of the performer, and not primarily as art, that it
is widely supposed that the participants are related and respond to one another as
in real-life situations. From the social angle it seems to be conceived of almost as an
exercise in, and sometimes even a test of, mutual adaptation and co-operation.
Preston-Dunlop, for example, whose helpful suggestions regarding the presentation
of Laban's themes of movement in *A Handbook for Modern Educational Dance*
(1963) seem to be based on the assumption that what is in hand is an aesthetic form
of understanding, nevertheless gives rise to doubts in this connection. She sees it
not only as "helping the child to become socially adapted," but as providing "an
excellent medium in which to develop satisfactory relationships with other
people" and (more explicit than most on this point), **boldly declares** modern
educational dance to be "nearer the life situation than the art situation" in this
respect.

When the promotion of "satisfactory relationships with other people" is spoken
of in this way, however, it is not at all clear what sort of relationships are in
question, and what is to count as satisfactory or unsatisfactory. What is particularly
debatable is whether the establishment of *personal* relationships is being claimed
and advocated. Obviously, a great deal of dance, both by its nature and as
practicable in schools and colleges, involves taking part with others. But in this it is
not alone. Drama, debates and most games, for example, also require other people
for the activity to proceed at all, and necessarily provide social experience at some
level. Even conflict and disagreement are essentially social in character; and to learn
how to participate in, say, a literary discussion, or in planning a geological
expedition, organising a concert or running a class magazine, is, by virtue of
becoming acquainted with the standards relevant to those pursuits, to become
socially adapted in an important sense. In so far as one learns how to function
efficiently as a chairman, a team leader or a stage manager, for instance, one could
be said to be developing "satisfactory" relationships with others.

Much more than this, however, or perhaps a difference not so much in degree as **Personal**
in kind, is generally thought to be achieved through dance, though the term **relationships**
"relationships" as applying to connections between people, is apt to be used
somewhat loosely in this sphere. Differences in the various types of relations that
may exist, according to whether those concerned are performing a dance, engaged
in the making of it, or are outside the context of dance altogether, tend to be
overlooked. (I myself have been as mistaken as any in this respect, and indeed
blatantly so, in stating that relationships in dance are "real and personal": see
Redfern, 1963). To fail to recognise these differences is to blur distinctions which
may well affect both the content and methods of dance teaching, as well as the
reasons adduced for the educational value of the subject.

It therefore behoves us to try to clarify our thinking on this point, and some assistance may be gained here from the chapter in Hirst and Peters (1970) on personal relationships (considered primarily in relation to teaching). Many profound and more detailed writings on this subject exist (see, for example, Macmurray, 1957, Polanyi, 1958, Buber, 1961, and Reid, 1961), but this text has been selected both on account of its recency and because it is almost alone in attempting to set out the necessary and sufficient conditions of the concept. As Hirst & Peters point out, "the term is a very vague one in ordinary use," and it seems easier on the whole to pin down what does *not* characterise a personal relationship than to provide it with positive content. Contrasting the word "relations" with "relationships" they find little distinction between the two furnished by everyday speech, but note that:-

'Relationship' suggests something more structured that grows up between or is entered into by the people concerned, and in which there is some element of reciprocity.

Further:-

This arises not from some impersonal order, whether of role, of convention or of morality, but from the initiative of the individuals concerned.

What is even more important than the content of a personal relationship, however, is the aspect under which it is viewed:-

The nearest we can get to characterising the positive attitude under which we view another, with whom we enter into a personal relationship, is brought out by words such as 'interest in' and 'concern for' another as a human being, together with some kind of openness or giving on one's own part. This must be a response to another *simply* as a human being, who is subject to pleasure and pain and the usual gamut of emotions and desires. In other words this attitude to another must not be connected with any extraneous purpose, whether individual or shared. He must not be thought of as a means to one's ends or just as a co-operator or competitor in a common pursuit.

In any curriculum activity, therefore, including dance, the relationships that exist as a direct result of the roles which those involved are called upon to play in the pursuit of that activity are to be distinguished from those of a personal variety. Individuals will collaborate, possibly argue, compete, share problems, reach solutions and make discoveries together, and so on, but all this will be because of some outside focus—whether the carrying out of a scientific experiment, the painting of a mural, or the making and performing of a dance. But, it might be objected, are not the participants in modern educational dance (and perhaps in some kinds of drama, too), by the very nature of the activity "interested in" and "concerned for" others as human beings, and not merely as co-dancers? Are they not related to one another precisely as members of the human race with personal feelings and desires, whose responses are part of the final "product"?

The reaction is predictable in the light of the common conceptions (or, rather, misconceptions), about expression and communication in relation to dance. It was pointed out earlier (section 2a) that expression theories of art are often linked with the idea of art as a language of communication—especially communication of feeling; but that since modern educational dance is held to be for the benefit of the performers, and not for spectators, communication must be thought to be between the participants themselves. As will be evident from what was said then, however, dance is not concerned with the revelation of the dancers' actual feelings to one another any more than to an audience, nor with the sharing of emotions and moods arising in response to real events and situations in the workaday world. What is communicated, in so far as feeling is of importance at all in a dance, is (to continue to use Langer's terms) "conceived" or "imagined" feeling; and if some aspect of the human condition is chosen as subject matter, it is *"presented,"* not brought into concrete existence. Neither is dance a sign-language, using movement as a substitute for words. Yawns, nods, pointings and other conventional gestures have no place in a symbolic form. So what are the performers "conversing" about? What sort of things do they communicate to one another through this medium?

It may sound somewhat strained and awkward to suggest that one dancer "states" in movement: "Look, here is a gradually decreasing spiral which speeds up at the end," and the other, "I can make one which complements yours—now we have created a pattern," and that the "conversation" thus proceeds; or that one, in performing a series of rhythmic steps and leaps, "announces" that he is advancing in lively fashion towards the other, who "replies" in similar vein, but by reversing the motif draws away from him. Put into words like this, the whole thing sounds rather absurd: what is missing is the very heart of the matter. The whole point of dance, as of any art form, is that what is conveyed is not reducible to other terms. A different medium, even a different arrangement of parts within the same medium, would have a different significance. Nevertheless, this is the *sort* of thing that can be said to be communicated in dance—even though it may not be conceived of in this way by the dancers themselves.* And this kind of communication is surely no less important than that concerning gossip about Sophia Loren's baby, or other casual verbal interchanges which might spark off an "embryonic" personal relationship (cf. Hirst & Peters).

Dance and communication

---

* It is indeed questionable whether, with children below, roughly, Middle School age, talk of "communication" in dance is really relevant. There seems rather to be growing awareness of how dancing with others can extend the possibilities of individual movement. Oakeshott (1962a), using the term "poetry" to stand for all artistic endeavour, describes one's young days as "a miraculous confusion of poetry and practical activity," when "we are moved not by the desire to communicate, but by the delight of utterance."

This applies whether the movement is set, or results from two individuals improvising within a given framework—for example, by taking it in turns to make a dance phrase related to the previous one by, for example, its shape, its bodily organisation, or its rhythmic-dynamic qualities. In the first case, they are like instrumentalists in an orchestra performing an already composed work in which, say, a tune is picked up from another section, answered with a variation, some embellishment, or a contrasting motif; in the second (when they might be more aware of the flavour of communication), they are more like jazz musicians extemporising. But in both cases participants in a dance, like musicians, communicate in terms peculiar to their own medium, which in turn determines *what* is communicated, and also makes for a quite special kind of relationship between them.

This, however, is different from the kind of exchange of thoughts and feelings that make for the establishing and cementing of *personal* ties with others. Dance is hardly a suitable medium for personal disclosures and the receivings of confidences, which Hirst & Peters suggest are a foremost feature of at least a fully-developed personal relationship, or for gaining knowledge "of the private lives of the people concerned and of their motives, attitudes and aspirations." Dancing with others and working out dances with them often provide fascinating insights into their temperament and character, but what is built up and shared is a different kind of world from that in which the business of ordinary living is carried on, and *as dancers* they can scarcely be said to be interested in one another as private individuals, each with his "particular and unrepeatable viewpoint on the world," in Peters' (1966) phrase. This difference is perhaps not so easy to appreciate when, as commonly happens in modern educational dance, dances are created by the dancers themselves on the basis of spontaneous interaction. As they experiment, pause to review progress, practise certain parts, discuss their efforts with the teacher, possibly demonstrate to other members of the class or break off to watch them in their turn, and so forth, there is a constant slipping in and out of the dance itself, a to-ing and fro-ing, as it were, between "reality" and the art situation, and this is apt to lead to an apparent merging of the two.

For a similar reason it might also be supposed that what is created in a dance is as much a private world as that involved in a personal relationship. But in spite of the fact that, as pointed out previously, the "material" of dance is the movement of living persons, not sound waves or inanimate substances, the dancers themselves do not *constitute* the dance. The two are separate entities, just as a piece of music is distinguishable from its performance. If it were otherwise, works such as "Giselle," "Revelations" or "Aureole" would have no permanence. They would simply cease to exist the moment that the dancers who originally danced them were no longer available—or, indeed, whenever they were not being performed. A dance, like any work of art, is an *actualisation of a possibility;* in common with a play, an opera or other musical work, it is (in technical language) a "type" of which there may be many "tokens" (cf. Charlton, 1970). As such it is public property. Even if, as is usually the case in the educational situation, the final form is not notated, it is *in principle* capable of being recorded, and can also be taught by other means to a different set of individuals. It thus has an existence independent of the particular occasion and the performers originally involved; a personal relationship, on the other hand, presupposes the uniqueness of those involved.

All this, of course, is not to deny that dance may *prompt* a personal interest in particular individuals just as human beings, nor that a closer relationship may develop as a result of the experience of dancing together (as may happen also whenever people associate for a common purpose and with a common interest). But there is no reason to suppose that should this not occur the enterprise has been a failure. It is obvious, too, that the subject-matter of some dance, and of much dance-drama, opens up insights into human relationships of a variety of kinds. Like literature and history, it may contribute a good deal to that form of knowledge which Hirst & Peters (1970) call "a most crucial form of understanding," i.e. interpersonal understanding. And this itself makes for an enrichment of personal relationships. *(margin: Dance and interpersonal understanding)*

Just as in literature and history comparisons may be drawn between events and human actions in fictitious circumstances or from the past and those within the first-hand experience of the pupils, so also in dance and dance-drama similarities are often noted between symbolic and real-life situations. But more than knowing *about* other people's relationships is involved in this form of understanding. Hirst and Peters insist that:-

> Interpersonal understanding is not a purely theoretical distanced form of knowledge. It involves imaginative reactions to what others will do, putting oneself in their shoes, seeing the world from their point of view as an arena for possible projects and predicaments.

This, as maintained in the essay in this volume on "Imagination" (see section 2), is exactly what is often demanded in modern educational dance (which, however receives no mention from Hirst & Peters).* But if interpersonal understanding may be gained, as they suggest, "by the taking of parts in drama, and by participation in games in which the intentions and plans of others have to be divined," then surely this applies in the case of dance.

Since during spontaneous group movement the participants are themselves actively involved in the creating, developing and resolving of "happenings," this would appear to be a peculiarly suitable occasion for the gaining of such understanding. In the main, of course, it comes about in informal situations outside

---

* Perhaps the latter is under the impression that it has to do with imagining that one is a leaf (*see* Peters, 1965).

the classroom, in connection with "projects and predicaments" of actual life. As Phenix (1964) points out, personal knowledge is "largely a product of ordinary social experience," not so much a matter of formal instruction as "a consequence of the basic fact of human association." Yet in modern educational dance, to choose between alternative courses of action and to make decisions such as whether to take the initiative, to follow or challenge the lead of another, or to act independently of a group or another person, is integral to that part of the scheme of training put forward by Laban which deals with partner and group work. Such contingencies require considerable attention to discerning the intentions and possible reactions of others, and are no less realities for taking place within the context of a symbolic and not a real-life situation. Even though these events make no difference to "the way the world is," and even if there is no carry-over of what is learned to ordinary life, the experience itself would seem to be not without value.

In addition, sensing and interpreting the responses of others to one's own actions contributes to one's understanding of oneself. In fact, according to Mead (1934), it is precisely through noting the reactions of others to one's own "gestures" (non-verbal and verbal), that one becomes aware of oneself in the first place. Whatever the validity of his theory that the self is not something which exists at birth and then enters into relationship with others, but develops through social interaction, there is undoubted merit in his suggestion that in situations involving "taking the attitude of the other" (imitative play, competitive games, and group activities generally), one comes to recognise how these "gestures" appear to others and how they judge them. Thus, by getting outside oneself, as it were, one sees oneself through their eyes. One also often becomes conscious of one's singularities (even idiosyncrasies) by contrast and comparison—for example, when trying to reproduce someone else's movement sequences, or conversely when one observes others making similar attempts in respect of one's own. Self-knowledge and knowledge of others seem to go hand in hand, and in education are of particular importance at adolescence, when young people are often concerned with problems of their own identity, and interested in how others—people they actually know, and not only characters in fiction or history—"tick."

Furthermore, there are implications of another kind in the fact that persons are not only "distinctive centres of consciousness" (Peters', 1966, phrase), but centres of consciousness linked with a physical body. Contrary to Langer's view that in dance all actualities disappear (cf.p.38 above), the performers are related in a very real way as they touch, hold, lift, swing one another around, synchronise their movements, vary their distance and so on. To appreciate that persons are embodied, and hence liable to suffer pain, is essential for moral understanding. But to refrain from hurting, or injuring or dealing roughly with another's body is to represent the negative side of the matter; a more positive aspect may be seen to include learning to act with care and sensitivity in establishing, or avoiding, physical contact.

Reid (1961), referring to those "who by some mischance have missed the opportunity of training in sense-discrimination" says:-

> In a half-empty bus on a hot day, they come and sit on top of you. They will clatter books and dishes; in a queue they push; if they drive a car they will jar the sensitive passenger, being without a certain kind of awareness of him or of mechanism.

He asserts moreover that "bodily insensitiveness can impoverish a whole outlook." Little, it seems, is done about this in education. Yet dance, and some aspects of physical education such as gymnastics and swimming, demanding as they often do that individuals learn to use and respond to touch, grip, pressure, support, and so forth, provide opportunities whereby discrimination of this kind may be developed. And it may sometimes not be inappropriate, in passing, to direct attention to its importance in other situations. In dance, of course, bodily contact, the distance between people and their being, for instance, opposite to each other, as compared with being side by side and having a common focus outside them, are of significance in themselves, and not only a practical expedient. A further dimension of understanding is thus involved: those of whom Reid speaks not only "may remain permanently clumsy in movement, insensitive to touch," but also be insensitive "to a world of symbolic meaning bound up with touch, and contact."

There are, then, a variety of objectives which might be achieved through the social aspects of modern educational dance, just as from the individual point of view there may be psychological satisfactions and reliefs (cf. p.83 above). But this does not render it a *branch* of moral or personal or interpersonal understanding, any more than in the latter case it becomes an off-shoot of psychotherapy, and it is of the utmost importance that any such results are recognised as by-products. This is not to underestimate their value, and they may constitute powerful reasons for according dance a firm place in the curriculum, but they cannot be the *aims* of the activity. Indeed it would be difficult to know how to proceed if they were conceived of in this way, for what would the participants set out to *do*? Commenting on Peters' (1966) argument in relation to games that if the players come to look on these activities as "exercises in morality, aesthetic grace, or in understanding others, they cease to be merely games, " Mollie Adams (1969) remarks:-

> Truly, one *cannot* play games, or paint pictures or whatever, looking to these virtues as objectives . . .

Even if, as she suggests, the educator regards them as *latent* objectives, the activity would become distorted as a result of trying to pursue it for these purposes.

Spontaneous adaptation and response to others is a perfectly legitimate means of approaching the composing of a partner or group dance, though, with the exception of young children with whom it may be inappropriate to press for selection and formulation, it is not the only, or necessarily the best way. (Indeed, large group dances sometimes seems to be more "creative" for the teacher than the dancers, as he watches from the outside for possibilities, seizes on chance happenings, decides on the retention of certain parts and the rejection of others, and so forth). But the dance lesson cannot become a time for a bit of social engineering. In his enthusiasm and concern (even anxiety) for group harmony, social adjustment and rewarding relationships, he may well lose sight of his initial task in dance, of initiating pupils into an aesthetic form of understanding. It is disastrous for aesthetic standards if considerations of the kind, "X hasn't had a turn at leading yet," are allowed to dominate the development of a composition. It is rather as if a composer of music were to think: "The second trombone has not had much to do so far—I'd better write a couple of dozen bars for him now." Of course such a state of affairs *might* be an indication that there is something structurally wrong with the composition, and obviously careful account must be taken of what individuals are capable of and what they are called upon to do in a dance. It is probably unlikely that it will be either a good dance, or a worthwhile experience for the person concerned, if he spends most of the time in some excruciating position, or else almost continually whirling round and round.

Whatever his discipline, the teacher has a dual concern: on the one hand for the standards which are characteristic of it, on the other, for those whom he seeks to make acquainted with those standards. If he is unsure of the criteria by which their achievements are to be judged and their progress assisted, he will fail on both counts. Similarly, the participants must not be left in any doubt as to what they are trying to achieve. Older children and students *might* conceivably be led to consider the latent objectives of dance in the educational setting, but during their involvement in the actual activity such considerations are not only irrelevant, but also likely to confuse and mislead. Maxine Sheets (1966) is one of the few writers on the subject alive to the dangers:-

> To overlook the labor and vital engagement necessary to the creation of a dance, and to concentrate instead on effective group interaction, individual growth, self-realisation, or whatever might come from such creation, is actually to nullify the dance . . . . When the concentration is on the student's social, intellectual, or emotional development, the student suffers because what she thinks she is doing is not what she is actually doing . . .

**Movement in everyday social life** What is not at all improbable, however, is that as a result of experience and study of dance, children and students may become interested (or interested in a more informed way than previously) in the significance of movement in everyday communication, and through their knowledge of the component elements of movement more skilled in observing the ways in which these are connected with personality and with moods of ordinary life. Laban (1948) seems to assume that this will happen as a matter of course. The essential distinction between expression and communication in art and non-art is once again ignored, and it is all too likely that a "capacity to communicate" is conceived of—another type of general ability like imagination, or bodily skilfulness, capable of development in some non-specific fashion:-

> As in all artistic activities, life experience is enhanced in dance through the concentration on definite rhythms and shapes of movement. The child becomes aware of the individualised entities of expression, which is an indispensable pre-requisite of the clearness and exactitude of any kind of expression and communication between people.

Even if this could be taken for granted (and it is no rare experience for teachers of modern educational dance to find older pupils and students commenting on their increased awareness of movement outside the dance situation), it might still be asked whether there is not a place in education for the study of movement specifically from this point of view, perhaps in conjunction with those aspects of sociology, social psychology and anthropology which focus on similar phenomena. Such a study would seem to be of particular importance in the training of teachers and others whose work involves a good deal of social interaction, and who might gain much from paying some attention to their own and others' "performances" in real-life situations. As indicated in the first of these essays, it is these, and not dance, which are relevant to this kind of investigation, and it should not be beyond the bounds of possibility to devise means of observing, for example, people engaged in discussion or an interview, carrying out a practical task, giving or being given instruction, and the like. That such an undertaking would require sensitive and imaginative handling is obvious, but this does not designate it an art activity. It would hardly be appropriate for it to be conducted in a clinical manner with members of the class studied as specimens or as case-book material; but it would be to the advantage of such a project *and* of dance, that they should be pursued independently, though this is not to say that experience gained from the one might not sometimes prove useful in the practice of the other.

To what extent, however, it would be necessary for purposes of this sort that students should engage in practical movement performance would be open to experiment. It might be thought unlikely that anything but a superficial understanding of movement could result from mere looking. This is just where what counts as "understanding" of movement in different areas is vital, and distinctions as to the different criteria relevant to the various situations in which movement plays a part. There is no *one* kind of movement understanding, and it neither follows logically, nor does it seem to work out in practice (though research is necessary to verify this), that acute observers are themselves skilled practitioners either in dance or any one kind of physical activity. Speaking of "the almost imperceptible expressive movements of hands, shoulders, and so on" (i.e. "shadow movements"), which would be of major significance in such a study, Laban &

Lawrence (1947) note:-

> To be a good observer of other persons' effort-expressions, one need not
> oneself have great bodily expressiveness. Good movers may be poor observers,
> and may even be unable to notice evident rhythm in larger movements.

Clearly, "creative dance" is not essential for this sort of study of movement;
learning to select and formulate movement as a structured art form is quite
different from learning to recognise the role it has in everyday communication.[*]

If modern educational dance were "nearer to the life situation than to the art
situation" in its social aspects, then canons of judgment of a kind different from
those of the aesthetic would apply. Presumably a set of values could be evolved to
establish what constitutes "good" and "poor" interaction and communication in
varied situations in real life. But if the participants are instead under the impression
that they are engaging in spontaneous adaptation as part of a process of composing
a dance, or with the object of becoming able to recognise movement "happenings"
which are capable of being developed along artistic lines, they might well succeed
according to criteria appropriate to these ends, but fare badly from the point of
view of a real-life encounter. Indeed, something more in the nature of an
"encounter group" might seem more suitable for such purposes. A pseudo-dance
situation can result neither in genuine personal interaction nor in the creation of an
art form.

We might do well in dance teaching, therefore, to think more about relations
between movements (including group movements), than about relationships
between persons. In any case, for any *latent* objectives to be realised such as those
mentioned above, it is necessary that the *primary* aims are achieved. If dance is
poor by aesthetic standards, it is hardly likely that it will succeed in education by
any other.

---

*For the same reason, it is not necessarily the teacher of dance, nor yet of drama, physical
education, or other activities in which bodily movement plays an obviously important part,
who would become a leader of such a project, though some might be recruited from these
ranks. Many questions arise as to the sort of training such a person would require, but this is not
the place to pursue them.

# C MODERN EDUCATIONAL DANCE

Section

## 4 PRINCIPLES OF MOVEMENT

---

**Principles of Movement**

The last feature of modern educational dance selected for the purpose of attempting to clarify this concept is that concerning "the principles of contemporary movement research," upon which Laban (1948) suggests that dance tuition is to be based.

As mentioned in the previous discussion of the "free" nature of the activity, and its claim to be "without a preconceived or dictated style," these two aspects are closely related (see pp.65 above.) That is, "free" does not imply a complete absence of order and guidance, dancing according to whim or the mood of the moment, but limited choice and response on the part of the performer within a planned framework. Ullmann (1960) writes:-

> In the contemporary art of movement we are not concerned with a particular style which has to be learned. It is, moreover, the study of fundamental principles and the challenge to the individual to respond and to create with them in his own personal way. This fact gives the modern approach to the art of movement a true educational standing.

Much therefore depends on the logical and epistemological status of these principles, more especially as they are held to apply to all movement. "The essential tool which can be offered to the educationist in modern dance," says Laban, "is the universal outlook upon the principles of human movement."

By "contemporary movement research" Laban means, it would seem, his work in industry, in particular the application of his "effort" theories, in collaboration with Lawrence. *(Modern Educational Dance,* 1948, followed on immediately after *Effort,* 1947.) It has already been noted that in the former it is stated:-

> The knowledge concerning human effort, and especially the efforts used by industrial man, is the basis of the dance tuition.

The significance for education of his industrial "research" lies, as Laban sees it, in the value of "effort training" both for promoting practical skilfulness of a general

117

kind and as a means of "harmonising" the personality. But as maintained in the essay on "effort" in this volume, neither of these claims can be substantiated: the former turns out to be untenable on empirical grounds, the second raises formidable problems of meaning. The sixteen basic movement themes, however, which form the basis of his scheme of dance training, are not confined to "effort" aspects (though these might be judged predominant), and in any consideration of Laban's movement principles the material of other themes must be taken into account as well.

It must also be remarked at the outset that Laban uses the term "research" in no generally accepted way. It lacks the standard reference which it has today in respect of investigations either of an empirical or a logical kind, namely, that of exhaustive and critical inquiry, the results of which are systematically recorded or set out as coherent arguments, and published so that they are available to others for checking and challenging. In Laban's usage it sometimes signifies little more than personal reflections and speculations about movement and dance, often of the sort which concern hidden values and meanings, and which attempt to penetrate the mysteries of the universe and of human life.

In the absence of concrete evidence, then, assertions which suggest a controlled, empirical approach (e.g. "the impact of movement on the mind has been studied and it has been found that . . .") have to be treated cautiously, especially in view of his tendency to sweeping statement. Moreover, the fact that such a subject is, at least in part, a matter for logical inquiry, goes unrecognised. Similarly, a claim such as that in respect of "what dancing or movement can really express," namely, that "in modern dance research this problem has been thoroughly investigated," reveals a lack of awareness that this is a philosophical problem shared by the arts in general. The extensive deliberations of others, however (generally of a far more scholarly and stringent kind than his own), are completely ignored; "thorough" investigation refers only to his own theorisings. As Curl (1969) observes, "Laban did not have the advantage of a rigorous scientific or philosophical training." He himself is quoted as saying: "I write not as a professional researcher but as a lay man" (Curl, 1967b).

Nevertheless this does not, of itself, preclude the possibility that his observations and speculations, or at least some of them, might yet be of value; and it is possible too that Laban's "principles" are not of the order, nor serve quite the same purpose, as he himself supposed.

To begin with, a distinction may be drawn between his *categorisation of movement* and his *underlying theories,* i.e. the fundamental assumptions forming the basis of his beliefs. Carlisle (1969), for example, is referring to the former when he says:-

The principles are not scientific in the hypothetico-deductive sense; rather it would seem that they have the functions of classification or description.

Curl, on the other hand, is speaking chiefly of the latter when he (1968a) states:-

> Laban's principles are Pythagorean—a mixture of myth, religion and mathematics.

This is not to say, of course, that there may not be a connection between the two. A classification represents a particular way of structuring some aspect of experience, and is not wholly to be divorced from certain presuppositions, interests and purposes. (The "fact/value" dichotomy is not, in fact, always as sharp as is sometimes maintained.) Nevertheless, a classification that one individual makes might be found to be relevant for other purposes, and employed and valued differently by other people.

It might next be asked what sort of a thing a "movement principle" might be. Laban himself uses the term, or a similar expression, comparatively rarely, and when he does this still leaves the matter in some doubt. When, for example, he (1948) refers to the "fundamental movement principle of kicking legs and hitting arms," this would appear to carry different implications from when he states that "there exists in the flow of man's movement some ordering principle which cannot be explained in the usual rationalistic manner." In many of his writings he speaks of "laws" and "rules" of movement, though in *Modern Educational Dance,* in addition to "principles," the term "technique" is often used, and with something of the force of the Greek *techne.* (Further reference to this will be made later.)

An easy answer is, in any case, precluded by the fact that the word "principle" is, in ordinary language, capable of a variety of usages. Often it is interchangeable with "law" or "rule," but sometimes this would be unusual or even incorrect. In logic, for example, there seems to be little difference between laws, rules and principles; but a *moral rule* is not the same thing as a *moral principle.* Again, we refer to the *law,* not the principle of gravity; but in the arts the tendency is to speak of *principles* of composition, less frequently of "laws" and "rules." A distinction which is vital, however, is that between *de*scriptive and *pre*scriptive laws. Among the former are so-called "laws of nature" which state what is, as matter of fact, always the case; they describe certain uniformities in nature, and have both explanatory and predictive functions. The latter, by contrast, lay down norms as to what should be done; unlike natural laws, which would still operate without man's presence in the universe (though their formulation is, of course, due to him), they involve specifically human activities and would cease to exist if mankind ceased to exist. Though they are fixed in one sense, they are not invariant as in the case of, say, the expansion of gases or the rate of acceleration of falling bodies. Like moral, economic or educational principles, they are connected with, and indeed arise from, particular enterprises in which some kind of order and structuring are thought necessary or desirable, and as values change, or it becomes expedient to do so, they may be altered or modified. Obviously *de*scriptive natural laws cannot be *pre*scriptive: Newton's laws of motion do not serve as injunctions or suggestions

"Laws" of movement

which may be followed or disregarded as thought fit. Rules on the other hand, are always *pre*scriptive. As Gottlieb (1968) observes:-

> It is pointless to provide by rule for something which is bound to happen anyway, for example to stipulate that 'breathing is compulsory'. Where things are physically necessary rules have nothing to accomplish. . . .

Put another way, prescriptive laws (and all rules)* are made, not discovered; descriptive laws are discovered, not made.

Laban, however, does not seem to have appreciated this fundamental difference. His talk of natural laws which "extend their influence far beyond the realm of purely physical and biological functions" is more characteristic of pre-scientific thinking than of one to whom "penetrating investigation into pure science" (Goodrich, 1956) is attributed. Yet often, in his talk of "laws" of movement, some of his most mystical notions jostle with ideas of a quite straightforward, easily understandable kind which have, moreover, obvious practical value. *Choreutics* (published in 1966, but based on a manuscript written in 1940), is a notable example of this. The opening chapters on "Principles of Orientation" and "The Body and the Kinesphere," for instance, like the chapter in *Modern Educational Dance* dealing with the same subject ("The Conception of the Sphere of Movement"), are in the main plainly descriptive. Granted that the dancer's need to be able to orientate himself is understood, any intelligent lay person would find little difficulty in grasping Laban's system for the division of space around the body. And the following statement might well be thought to be dealing with principles of harmony as in music:-

> Knowing the rules of the harmonic relations in space we can then control and form the flux of our motivity.

Such controlling and forming would probably be interpreted as having relevance for dance invention in the way that the relations between sounds are studied for the purpose of musical composition. But considerable puzzlement would be likely to arise in connection with what ensues:-

> This science of harmonic circles has its origin in the discovery of the laws which rule the architecture of the body. It is obvious that harmonious movement follows the circles which are most appropriate to our bodily construction.

---

* cf. also Wittgenstein (1953):-
    The word 'agreement' and the word 'rule' are *related* to one another; they are cousins. If I teach anyone the use of the one word, he learns the use of the other with it.

"Laws which *rule* the architecture of the body"? What sort of laws can these be? "Harmonious movement"—has the discussion now shifted to anatomical functioning—what is easy, or pleasant, to do bodily? Is the purpose after all mainly physical, some special sort of "keep fit"? And when, in conclusion, it is stated as a "fact of space-movement" that:-

Our body is the mirror through which we become aware of ever-circling motions in the universe with their polygonal rhythms

Laban's concepts are likely to be dismissed as "mystical pseudo-science" (Adams, 1969).

When Laban speaks in this vein, his "principles" are clearly not *prescriptive*, i.e. serving as *guides for procedure and practice* as in the case of principles of harmony and composition in music. And yet neither are they *descriptive* in the scientific sense. Indeed he constantly stresses the inadequacy of principles of mechanics for an understanding of human movement. It is bodily movement in all its psychosomatic richness, and not merely, or even primarily, the body as a physical entity that he is concerned with. But the "laws" which he has in mind in describing it are those of growth and change, as in the life of plants and in processes of crystallisation, and the rhythms of tides and seasons and the stars in their courses. In "The Rhythm of Living Energy" (1959) he writes:-

Our mobility is one and indivisible . . . and follows a unique line of rules which conform to atomic or astral movement as well as to crystallisation, organic growth and inner life and consciousness.

Such laws cannot govern bodily movement, however. Laws of nature, unlike man-made laws, are not of the kind which can be obeyed or broken, whereas obviously a person can choose to order the rhythms and pathways of his movement in any way that he likes (within, of course, the bounds of his bodily mobility). Indeed Laban frequently deplores that in doing just this, "civilised" man neglects, or refuses, to follow those which he *ought.* This is no prudential "ought." It has, in fact, moral force, as is clear from "The Importance of Dancing" (1959):-

In dancing as in doing there exists a formidable order and common code of laws without which life becomes meaningless, if not evil . . . these laws are given by nature and . . . (man) as controller-servant can do nothing but recognise and cultivate the pre-established harmony.

There is thus radical confusion. These "laws" of dance are first presented as having *descriptive* status—yet since the movement of human beings does not invariably conform to them they obviously are not laws of nature; they therefore become *prescriptive*, laying down what man *ought* to do: he is viewed as owing moral allegiance to an almost divine order.

Although nothing of all this is explicit in *Modern Educational Dance* there are nevertheless unmistakable echoes of it from time to time. It would indeed be strange if it were otherwise; right up to the time of his death Laban was writing and speaking of "the invariable rules of bodily and mental motion" (1957), "the world of rhythm and harmony" (1958a) and so on. The "ordering principle which cannot be explained in the usual rationalistic manner," to which he refers in the Introduction, is none other than the "natural lawfulness" of which we hear much more elsewhere; and the "innate urge of children to perform dance-like movements," which the educationist is enjoined to preserve and cultivate, is that "mysterious compulsion" which is obeyed by all undegenerate creatures that do not suffer from "a misinterpretation of natural laws through the pertness of (our) intellect" (see 1959c).

Moreover, while Curl (1967b) is probably right that Laban's "philosophical foundations" are "only vaguely recognised in present-day practice," they have nonetheless a marked influence on that practice in those cases where dance is pursued not primarily as an aesthetic discipline, but as an activity in which the "impressive" aspects of movement are stressed, and the experience of the doer rated above all else. For it is by following "natural" sequences of movement which allegedly accord with the rhythms and patterns of nature that, in Laban's view, the human being attains certain states of mind; and its educational value is seen essentially in its power to "harmonise" and "unify" the personality through his thus becoming in tune with the cosmos.

**Laban's classific- ation of movement**    Enough, however, has been said to show that neither the content of Laban's "principles" in this sense, nor his justification for their adoption, can be reckoned worthy of serious consideration in education. But we may well ask, with Curl (1969):-

If the objective cosmological status of Laban's ideas is discredited, does there not remain some significant qualitative value that would account for the sensitive work we have witnessed in schools and colleges in this country?

And the answer would seem to be that it is his principles of movement *in the classificatory sense* that is important, and that if the actual *movement* material is divorced from many of the "explanations" and suppositions attaching to them, a substantial body of ideas is to be found which are of immediate relevance and usefulness for both the theory and practice of dance *as an art.*

Laban was, after all, nothing if not a practitioner, and the substance of the sixteen basic movement themes (though considerably condensed and simplified in the form in which these are set out in *Modern Educational Dance*), is remarkably down-to-earth and comprehensive. Expanded and explained in greater detail, as in

Preston-Dunlop's *A Handbook for Modern Educational Dance* (1963), as well as in practice over the years in his classes and those of his associates (in particular, Lisa Ullmann, Director of the Art of Movement Studio), and supplemented by suggestions for its application in schools by several authors,* it has formed the key-stone for much of the "sensitive work" to which Curl refers. And Laban's dance notation, which has achieved widespread recognition, exemplifies the validity of his analysis of movement in terms of the flow of the parts of the body, with varying degrees of exertion, in space and time.

What is crucial for composing, performing *and* the appreciation of dance as an art form is that the pupil/student learns to deal with *movement* ideas, through becoming progressively acquainted with the component elements of movement which are comparable with the rudiments to which he is introduced in music. Just as he would be lost in a meaningless welter of sound if there were no basis for discriminating such things as intervals, chords, rhythmic units and such like, so the general flux of movement would be impossibly blurred and incomprehensible if there were no means of marking out distinctions and relations which enable him to find his way about, so to speak. And this is precisely what Laban's categorisation provides. Moreover, it is not sufficient merely to pick out *single* constituents; the student of dance has to be helped also to perceive and respond to the ways in which rhythmical elements and shapes in space are related and structured. Again, Laban's description is more than a breaking down into separate parts; it involves a systematisation of rhythmic compounds and space-forms: hence the dominating concept of the *flow* of movement.

The concern of Modern Dance (on both sides of the Atlantic) with this flow has already been noted (cf. section 1), but probably no one is more identified with the term than Laban. Although he uses it in a variety of ways, ranging from the simple idea of the progression of movement through time, to notions of some mysterious factor of spiritual significance (often in these cases associated with his metaphysical concepts of unity and harmony), this should not blind us to the importance of the conception of movement as a *process of change,* the nature of which can be observed, described and recorded once a basis for distinguishing movement constituents has been established. It would thus be unwise to overlook the value of certain aspects of Laban's "effort" and "space harmony" ideas, even though the tenets associatied with them are unacceptable; a promising infant must not be thrown out with the Pythagorean bathwater.

As indicated in the previous essay (B), it is possible to dispense with the notion of "effort" as an inner function or faculty which can be trained, together with the related concepts of "effort balance" and "effort harmony" where these carry metaphysical implications, yet appreciate the significance for dance of Laban's

---

*Notably, Russell (1958; 1965; 1969), Carroll & Lofthouse (1969) and Preston-Dunlop (1963) herself.

codification of so-called "effort elements," "effort compounds" and "effort transitions." Dance cannot be practised or understood without insight into its rhythmical features, and a valuable contribution to ways of organising and developing this aspect of study, especially perhaps where "free" rhythm is concerned, is afforded by Laban's recommendations regarding the releasing and arresting of flow, the control of tension and relaxation, of dynamic stresses of varying shades of intensity, of differentiated time qualities, of increase and decrease of energy and speed, and so forth.

Similarly, it is not necessary to subscribe to the idea that through certain spatial configurations one can achieve unity with the cosmos, in order to recognise the usefulness of Laban's system of "space harmony" (or "choreutics"). Through this there is available to the dancer a means of sorting out and developing shapes and patterns within the maze of pathways which evolve on the floor and in the air as he "perambulates or whirls about" as Laban (1958a) puts it; and of mapping out the space surrounding him (the "kinesphere") so that he may not only orientate himself securely within it, but also become familiar with the relationships between various points of orientation and between the pathways ("trace-forms") which are thus created.

*"Harmony" in this sense has to be distinguished from the idea of the "harmonising" effect of dance upon the personality.* It refers instead (and this is how Preston-Dunlop, 1963, presumably understands the term), to a study of the proportional relations of movements in space comparable with those between sounds as they are studied in music. Thus sequences having regular order may be worked out on a basis similar to that of the harmonic progression of tones and chords. In the words of the 1963 edition of *Modern Educational Dance:-*

> There is a logical order underlying the evolutions of the various shapes in space which can be realised in scales. Scales are graduated series of movements which pass through space in a particular order of balancing tensions according to a specified scheme of relations of the spatial inclinations.

Such scales and other sequences of movement, however, are to be practised not because we believe that "choreutics attempts to stop the progress of disintegrating into disunity" (Laban, 1966), i.e. in the psychological or metaphysical sense, but because it can bring order out of chaos in *aesthetic* terms. It is both a means of training the performer and a guide in composition.

In the latter connection it is worth pausing to consider how it is that works of art are objects of the so-called "distance" senses (i.e. hearing and sight), but not of taste, smell or touch (cf. Prall, 1936). Although attempts have been made to organise the objects of these "contact" senses into aesthetic wholes, they appear to have failed largely because there is no means of establishing exactly specifiable relations between gustatory or olfactory or tactile ("feel") qualities. There is no precise way of comparing, for example, the fragrance of pine trees with the smell of rancid butter, the taste of honey with the flavour of kippers, the feel of velvet with that of glue. Resinous is not on any sort of continuum with putrid, sweet with salty, or smooth with sticky, and so on. There is thus no foundation for ordering and structuring *intelligible patterns* as in the case of auditory and visual perceptions. There have to be distinguishable *gradations* of similarity and contrast; not simply variation, but a basis for systematic variation.

In music, sounds are related to one another in respect of their pitch, intensity and timbre, and in the visual arts exact comparisons can be made in respect of hue, saturation and "brightness" of colour, and of angles and shapes of lines, surfaces and masses. In dance, however, while a recognisable range of energy and speed of movement has long facilitated the development of rhythmical aspects, a comparable basis for systematic spatial development has been lacking. This probably accounts very largely for the predominance of expressionist and representational forms of dance; composition along formal lines has been chiefly (especially in classical ballet) by a process of re-arrangement and what Selden (1930) calls "accretion." But if relations between directions and pathways are established in a logical fashion, as in Laban's system of "space harmony," this difficulty can be overcome—or, at least, one possible solution is provided. By such means, new ways of composing are opened up and a further dimension brought to the evaluation of dance works.

It is not, however, as Curl (1968a) seems to imply, a matter of laying down an arbitrary mathematical formula for beauty, of trying to calculate the value of a dance in measureable terms. It is, rather, as Charlton (1970) suggests, a question of taking into account the relations between perceptible qualities which are "particularly well adapted to being perceived." Aesthetic pleasure, he argues, consists not so much in having pleasant sensations as in the *activity* of looking and listening attentively, and this is to be characterised as *following a process of change.* This involves knowing, so to speak, where we are, which in turn calls for perceiving relations between qualities—pitches, angles, shapes, etc., and looking or listening for *developments.* And a work of art, he maintains, succeeds by formalist criteria (though these are not always the most appropriate by which to judge some works), insofar as its pattern of sounds or shapes is easy to follow.* Expectations are aroused and we are gratified, surprised and so on, as these expectations are fulfilled or delayed or disappointed. Further, what are most easily followed are patterns whose qualities are proportionally related to one another. In the case of following a visual pattern he writes:-

---

* This does not imply that works of art do not contain "variety, surprises, even some difficulty." But the unexpected is *understandable* insofar as the listener or viewer is able to "supply fairly technical descriptions of what is happening..." In the case of music for example:-
> The fuller and deeper descriptions a hearer can supply, the better he follows the music, and, we may suppose, if he follows it without effort, the more he enjoys it.

How can such elements be related? There is only one way possible: quantitatively. A distance, area, or angle may be equal to, or some multiple or fraction of, another. So it is relations of this sort which must be clear. A pattern has unity insofar as the beholder can tell how great each distance, angle, etc. is, not absolutely, but in relation to the others.

The theory of proportion is therefore far from defunct in current aesthetic debate, and Charlton's later references to the significance of mathematical relations in sound and visual pattern are full of interest for the student of Laban's choreutic ideas. It might almost be Laban speaking when Charlton says:-

A spiral, in which the various parts are related in a steady, simple way, may be compared with a scale in music . . . . We have modes and keys, and the key of C major, or the Greek Lydian mode, has a sort of primacy in music. In the same way we have qualitatively different spirals as the angle or curvature or the ratio of successive sides varies; and a ratio central to visual design seems to be that of $\sqrt{5}$-1:2. This is the so-called Golden Section . . . Rectangular and curved spirals based on it are generally considered highly satisfactory.

Osborne (1968), commenting on the same subject, observes:-

Such a canon might have aesthetic significance, as the ancient tradition seems to have supposed, by helping to ensure *a principle of organic unity* throughout the whole art work (my italics).

There are, it is true, serious difficulties about the notion of "organic unity" as the distinguishing feature of works of art (see, for example, Macdonald, 1951), but to say that they share "a common quality of unified complexity, or self-contained wholeness" need not, Sonia Greger (1969) maintains, amount to a tautologous definition. By examining "the many differential ways in which the elements of an art form can 'mean'," and how "such different functions work together to form, not isolated parts cemented together . . . into an enforced unity, but a *system* in which parts are meaningfully related," and in which different sets of relationships operate, she illustrates "an essential quality in the functioning of art forms: namely their capacity to cohere, or hold together."

In dance, such coherence depends at least in part on the way in which its spatial elements are related, and though Laban (somewhat surprisingly, it might seem, in view of his being so strongly associated with "expressive" dance), adopts an extreme formalist position when he (1956) says that "the development of a movement idea through different logical stages is nowadays the only true criterion of the worth of a dance," he is supplying a very necessary counter-balance to those accounts of dance which lean heavily on expressionist and representational considerations. The scales and "rings" and other sequences which Laban formulated, and which involve sets of proportional relationships between movements based on a geometric division of space appropriate to the structure of the body are not, however, for wholesale transporting into dance composition in a stereotyped form any more than is the case with scales in music, although in both art forms parts of such series may be taken as *units* of composition. They also provide typically thematic material for *dance-studies,* in a way similar to that in which, say, octaves, arpeggios or consecutive thirds may constitute the basis of a piano étude. In addition, they likewise have for the performer the value of presenting particular challenges of a technical kind, such as maintaining stable equilibrium, mastering the fluency and transiency of diagonally-stressed move-ment, or of constantly changing the inclination of the body without giving up balance completely.

Such formulations are, however, *constructions* rather than *discoveries*—a product of the human mind, with its capacity to organise and structure experience. There are not, and never were, pre-existing pathways and ideal harmonies of movement waiting "out there" to be found and followed. But Laban's choreutics is none the less remarkable for that. Indeed, as a "creative device" (Curl's phrase), rather than, as Laban himself supposed, an uncovering of facts of nature, it is more relevant to the dance than the accumulation of data of the kind which yield scientific laws. Whether, as a matter of historical fact (and there might of course have been an interaction of the two factors), Laban began from an empirical standpoint, observing bodily construction and the zones of space into which each limb appears to reach most easily, or whether, as Curl (1968a) surmises, he fitted everything into a Pythagorean scheme of proportion because of its alleged cosmological significance, does not seem to matter a great deal from the point of view of the practical implications of his system. * What is important is that here we have a means of ordering movements in space for the purposes of dance which takes account of the structure of the human body and the way it can move.

Even if another system were worked out, Laban's understanding of the need for such ordering is itself worthy of recognition: his conception of the "kinesphere" alone is of considerable value. Presumably, however, so long as allowances are made for what is physically possible, different divisions of space could be devised, giving other pathways and relations between them. In music there are other systems of harmony besides that based on the diatonic scale which, as Curl (1968b) points out, "carries no absolute law." But as he also remarks, this has led to the establishment of a great tradition. Without it the development of music in the West would have been seriously handicapped, and in the absence of any comparable system for ordering and developing the spatial elements of movement, it would be somewhat shortsighted to ignore completely what has already been evolved, and to

---

* This is not to suggest that an understanding of his "philosophical foundations" is unimportant, however. Indeed, it is necessary for making sense of much that is otherwise puzzling in his writings.

rely exclusively, as often seems to happen in dance composition, on intuitive or hit-and-miss methods. Laban himself, for all his apparent stress on spontaneity and freedom of expression, has no illusions on this score when it comes to dance as an art, which, he (1956) says:-

> ... cannot be based on spontaneous improvisations only. Movement compositions, as well as poetry and music, have to be carefully constructed and built up according to the general rules of artistic composition.

It is, of course, rather ironic that a basis for the formal structuring of dance should become available in an age which tends to overthrow order in art as in much else, which seems to prefer noise to sound, formlessness to design, irregularity to regularity. Yet in each case a concept of the former presupposes a concept of the latter, and many twentieth-century developments in music and art have been possible only because of traditional ideas and techniques dependent on a grasp of mathematical rules. Even if these are broken, they provide, as it were, a jumping-off place; they are always "there," so to speak, in the background. Clark (1956) writes:-

> Although the artist cannot construct a beautiful nude by mathematical rules, any more than the musician can compose a beautiful fugue, he cannot ignore them. . . . Ultimately he is as dependent on them as an architect.

And as he further observes:-

> Since art is concerned with sensory images the scale and rhythm of the body is not easily ignored. Our continuous effort, made in defiance of the pull of gravity, to keep ourselves balanced upright on our legs affects every judgment on design, even our conception of which angle shall be called "right."

Perhaps then, paradoxically, what is a well-established basis of practice in other arts might be innovatory in the dance, and a necessary preliminary to future developments in respect of formalist considerations.

So far, however, the possibilities of Laban's "space harmony" have been exploited to only a relatively small extent, though they would seem to be at least of equal, if not greater, importance for dance than his "effort" principles. In general, more significance has been accorded to these than to his choreutic ideas, though the reasons for this become clearer when his own account of "educational" dance, and the appeal of "the development of the personality" thesis is appreciated. In addition, it has to be remembered that much secondary school work at the present time is in the hands of teachers of physical education, whose own level of skill and understanding in the area of "space harmony" is often not very high. The situation might, of course, be reversed if the tradition had been to lay stress on the *making of dances,* rather than on the *experience of dancing,* and if dance appreciation were built into the total programme of dance education as an essential element.

Touching this point, an important consequence of the continuous ordering of sensory elements may be noted, namely, that aesthetic judgments made in respect of particular structures of these (i.e. art works) is thereby rendered susceptible to rational debate. It becomes possible to offer reasons in support of claims about their aesthetic value which is just not feasible in the case of, for example, the scent of this rose rather than that, this taste or "feel" rather than another. All that can be stated in these instances seem to be purely personal preferences: comparisons and contrasts are not in terms of the object itself, but wholly of one's private experiences. Yet it has to be admitted that, both in the theatre and in education, much critical appraisal remains at a deplorably low level—on the one hand, approximating to gasps of delight and grunts of disapproval, on the other, dealing mainly with extrinsic considerations. There may be intelligent assessment of the performers' technical accomplishments,* discriminating comment on décor, costume, lighting, and such like, intense interest in the sources of inspiration and the bringing into being of the dance. But any discussion of the substance of the dance itself, and in particular of its formal qualities, is often conspicuous by its absence, or else glossed over, or largely irrelevant. Concentration is often on any narrative element the work may have, or its "meaning" in terms of its reference to events and conditions of life *outside* dance, while a readiness to treat it as an "interpretation" of music is still not unknown. [right margin: *Movement principles and dance criticism*]

The great merit of Laban's principles (taken in the sense of his categorisation of movement) is that they focus attention on the *material* of dance, and provide a basis for dealing with this. In Wigman's (1959) words:-

> Movement—in all its possibilities and varieties, in its utmost simplicity as well as in its intricate extravagance . . . movement and movement again—that is the extraordinary thing Laban gave back to the dance, so that once more we can understand and experience it, can read, write and speak it as an artistic language of its own.

This possibility of learning the "language" of dance, and not simply one of the many dance "languages," has implications of the highest importance for the subject as an educational activity. Training in one specific form of dance (e.g. classical ballet, Sword dancing or Revived Greek Dance), may require attention to the rudiments of movement insofar as aspects of these are exemplified in the idiom [right margin: *Movement principles and educational implications*]

---

* "Technical" in the limited, though not, of course, unimportant sense of bodily skill. As will be clear from the foregoing, however, rhythmic and spatial sensitivity is also properly thought of as constituting mastery.

concerned, but it need not involve a comprehensive study of them in their own right. Though becoming well acquainted with, perhaps even expert in, one corner of the whole domain of dance, the learner may well remain ignorant not only of other corners, but also of what *constitutes* this domain. He is in a situation somewhat comparable to that of one who takes blank verse to be the whole of poetry, or plainsong the sum total of music. Without some means of gaining access to an overall view, he is likely to find much dance wholly unintelligible, and his ability to form independent judgments will be limited. It is therefore difficult to see how such a procedure can be considered educational.

What is necessary is that the student of dance in a school or a college is equipped to recognise what *makes* for a style, how it represents (albeit at an unconscious level) a selection of the vast range of movement possibilities available to the human being; and that in gaining a broad perspective—a means for what Laban (1948) calls "conscious penetration into the jungle of dance forms"—he learns to exercise discrimination, to make choices of his own, and to develop his own style of composing and performing.

This would seem to be most capable of achievement through a scheme based on movement concepts fundamental to dance (rhythm and phrasing, shape and pattern, etc.), and which marks out types of group formation and of movement relationships between individuals and groups. Laban's proposals, as summarised in the sixteen basic movement themes, which meet these requirements (though they might be thought to need supplementing with more details of training the body from a purely physical point of view), should not, however, be regarded as the blueprint for all time—nor, indeed, judging by Laban's own remarks were they intended as such. But they might be taken to illustrate the *kind* of scheme required. There is no reason why they have to be adopted just as they stand (many practitioners, while retaining his general classification already reject the thematic approach), nor why Laban's plan should not be modified in other ways, and developed and used in conjunction with other systems which seek to further understanding of the elements of movement relevant to dance, and to stimulate new ways of composing and looking at dance.

This, moreover, is what constitutes the main theoretical content of the subject. Whatever else is studied, such as the history of dance, musical accompaniment, sociological aspects and so forth, the student's major concern is with movement ("the elemental and incontestable basis without which there would be no dance," in Wigman's, 1966, phrase), with its analysis and recording, and with its organisation and development as an art form. It is interesting in this connection that Laban, who in some ways might seem to stand for all that is anti-intellectual and non-academic in the field of dance education, places a grasp of underlying principles, alongside the preserving and strengthening of the child's tendency to engage in dance-like movement, as a primary aim:-

The first task of the school is to foster and to concentrate this urge, and to make the children of the higher age-groups conscious of some of the principles governing movement.

And in *Modern Educational Dance* (especially the introductory chapter), his use of the term "technique," which is otherwise almost incomprehensible in some contexts, seem to make most sense when taken as meaning much the same as the Greek *techne* from which it is derived, i.e. *knowledge* of the kind which is capable of precise formulation, as contrasted with non-specifiable "know-how" or "knack" (cf. Oakeshott, 1962b). In other words, the supposition seems to be that something more than a set of practical skills is desirable—namely, an understanding of the rationale underlying those skills; and such a systematisation of knowledge is what Laban sets out to provide.

A further point concerned with "principles of movement" is that whatever is selected as the *content* of a dance syllabus also determines in some measure *methods* and *manner* of dance teaching. Just as a verbal language is learned partly by listening to others speak, partly by trying to repeat exactly what they say and how they say it, and partly by struggling to formulate one's own phrases and sentences, so an understanding of the "language" of dance is gained by a comparable variety of means—by watching performances, by practising set sequences, studies etc., and by attempting to compose oneself. Some of these ways may well prove more appropriate at some stages than at others, but concentration on one to the exclusion of the rest constitutes an inadequate dance programme. In the past modern educational dance has been apt to underestimate the importance of the first two, especially perhaps dance appreciation; but it is no accident that dance "without a preconceived or dictated style" lays stress on the third aspect—is, indeed, "creative" dance, and in being centrally concerned with principles of movement, provides, as Ullmann (1960) says, a challenge to the individual "to respond and to create with them in his own personal way."

Not everyone is likely to be able to create major dance works, but in structuring even short sequences the learner comes to grips with the material of his art in a way similar to that in which, in music, knowledge is both achieved and exemplified by composing a few bars based on a given selection of musical ideas. And, as he progresses, the practice and understanding of a wide range of movement enables him, as already pointed out (cf. p.68 above), to deal with a variety of themes and ideas, kinetic and non-kinetic. He thus becomes "free" in an important sense, sharing that privilege of the twentieth-century generation of dancers who, in Sachs' (1937) words, "build freely on the happy consciousness of the body."

What they dance is as manifold as their temperaments—serious and gay, stately and playful, earthbound and heaven-storming, simple and grotesque, crude and refined, human and demoniacal. (Sachs, 1937).

It is pertinent too from the educational standpoint to recognise that, as Scheffler (1965) points out, rational autonomy is not confined to the sphere of propositional knowledge, but extends also to the realm of practical skill. It is hardly likely, however, where the programme consists of training in specific styles of dance only, that a critical attitude will be fostered as regards the following of certain procedures rather than others, and the preferring of certain kinds of subject matter. The ability and readiness to experiment boldly may therefore be inhibited and the implicit value placed on the style in question, along with the particular skills it involves, will tend to go unchallenged.

If what goes on in the name of dance in schools and colleges encourages the assumption that one form of dance or one type of technique is indisputably superior to another, and results in the learner being ignorant of and unsympathetic to other outlooks, dependent on this authority or that, unwilling to try out for himself methods and procedures different from those to which he is accustomed, then far from being educational, this comes near to a kind of indoctrination.

What Powell (1967) has to say about the acquisition of sophisticated capacities such as inventiveness, originality, creativeness, resourcefulness, and the like, applies also to the development of skill in the realm of dance:-

> Thinking can be conducted in a routine, derivative, stereotyped and imitative fashion . . . . A good deal of teaching consists of (such) demonstrations coupled with the injunction 'Do it like this'. But if the teacher concludes by asking whether the student thinks that the demonstrated technique is in any way defective and invites him to indicate ways in which it might be improved, then he is encouraging him to be creative—and critical. For to be critical of performances is, in part, to suggest new ways in which they could be carried out and thus to create new ways of performing.

It seems, in fact, unlikely that skills which involve an element of novelty can be taught, and, as Powell maintains, all that can be done is to put the learner in the way of working in the desired manner. This means that "he must have a base from which to extend himself in creative directions. . . . For one must have some command of the routine and the familiar in order to go beyond it."

It is, however, a cardinal error to suppose that what is a base for skill and creativeness in dance provides also an appropriate base for creativeness and skill in other fields, whether in the other arts or in activities requiring gross physical movement. This raises the issue of the universal applicability of Laban's "movement principles" and his all-embracing conception of "the art of movement."

It is clear that for the art form of dance there is a need for a comprehensive system of classifying movement, and an attempt has been made in the foregoing pages to illustrate the relevance and importance of that proposed by Laban. It has also been argued that the teaching of dance in a manner befitting an *educational* activity demands some such categorial scheme. What is far less certain, however, is not simply whether Laban's analysis is adequate for all human movement, but whether any one system could be. It is not so much a question of the *possibility* of describing any sort of movement in a particular set of terms, as what the *point* of this would be. Since bodily movement fulfils a host of different purposes, it may be viewed under a variety of aspects, and no single description is likely to prove universally valuable. Just as an account from the anatomical angle, for instance, is of little use for the understanding of a dance, so a classification suitable for the art form of movement may be largely irrelevant for other kinds.

It is no doubt salutary for us all from time to time to pause and consider the immense significance of movement in our lives—and when older children and students are first helped to do so they often find it an impressive fact. But to conceive of it as a uniform, undifferentiated phenomenon, to imagine that activities as widely diverse as stage performance of all kinds, social dancing, rituals and ceremonies, public speaking, games and working operations can be bound together into a logical unity, "the art of movement," that they are governed by the same set of principles and may profitably be practised by reference to one "technique of moving," is not to illuminate but to confuse. Models of description and explanation of the over-arching, all-inclusive kind, whether in respect of knowledge, activity, behaviour or skill, while perhaps seeming at first blush to simplify and synthesise, in fact often prevent an understanding of connections and relationships because fundamental distinctions are ignored or unrecognised. They frequently involve what Ryle (1949) calls "category mistakes."

If we take

> The dance along the artery
> The circulation of the lymph
> Are figured in the drift of stars

> (T.S. Eliot: Burnt Norton)

as a scientific proposition, and not a poetic statement, this is to mistake one "voice" in the "conversation of mankind" for another, to try to play one "language-game" according to the rules belonging to a different one (cf. p.78 above): in short to be a victim of myth. *This sort of slide occurs persistently with Laban who, as Curl, drawing on Langer, observes, "fails to distinguish

---

* cf. Ryle (1949):-
   A myth is, of course, not a fairy story. It is the presentation of one category in the idioms appropriate to another.

between 'physical fact' and 'artistic significance', between 'symptom' and 'symbol', between 'nature' and 'art' . . . "(Curl, 1968a).

To propose, for example, a scheme of mathematical proportions between movements in space for the purpose of dance is one thing; to move over to propounding that "there exists an almost mathematical relationship between the inner motivation of movement and the functions of the body" (Laban, 1950 Preface) is quite another. And when this leads to the conclusion that "guidance in the knowledge of the common principles of impulse and function is the only means that can promote the freedom and spontaneity of the moving person," practice is likely to be misguided.

The study of movement is such a vast subject, even when it is restricted to that of human beings, that to attempt to undertake it at all without clear specification of the particular angle(s) from which it is to be viewed might well seem a daunting, if not a pointless, enterprise. There is no one domain, "movement knowledge" or "movement understanding"; neither is there such a thing as "movement training" of a general kind. One cannot practise "just moving." The differing functions which bodily movement may serve, especially taking into account the particular intentions and aims of the agent, call both for different ways of looking at the movement involved and for means of training specific to whatever activity is in hand. An actor, for instance, is hardly likely to benefit *as an actor* from the same sort of training in movement as that designed for trampolining. The idea of a "dance technique promoting the mastery of movement in all its bodily and mental aspects" (Laban, 1948) is without substance.

Yet there is still talk of "movement experience" and of "knowing movement" (see, for instance, North, 1971);* and the idea (at its most popular in the 1950s), that something in the nature of "basic movement" exists, which can somehow be extracted from its context, practised in isolation and then, as it were, put back, dies hard in educational circles. A typical statement from a non-specialist, but a former member of H.M. Inspectorate writing about "body and soul" in the primary school, is that of Blackie (1967), who prefaces his consideration of "what is usually described as Movement, with a capital M," as he calls it, with the modest remark that "it is not easy to describe a Movement session to someone who has not seen one . . .":-

> The object of Movement in school is to provide a basic training in control of the body so that all movements may be improved and so that the specialised movements required for particular sports and crafts may be more easily learned.

---

* Often, however, these terms function as persuasive definitions (see Stevenson, 1944), containing a disguised recommendation that a particular form of movement understanding, (unstated, but intelligible as dance understanding rather than anything else), is the 'true' kind or the only one worth pursuing.

Although with young children, as the Plowden Report (1967) points out, it is not easy "to separate different modes of movement experience," it is more a case of their slipping quickly and frequently from one type of activity in which movement plays a major part to another, than of there being a homogenous entity "movement." Movement as activity cannot be engaged in in a vacuum, and in education the notion of foundation courses of a practical nature which are then meant to branch out into dance, drama, or some physical education activity, of classes which are supposed "lead to" this or that, is utterly misconceived. One cannot *approach* what already consists of movement used for a distinct purpose *via* some vague mishmash labelled "movement." One can only get going with movement within a frame of reference, *relating* it, and paying attention, as appropriate, to whatever features it is relevant to take into account for the success of the pursuit in question.

When reference is made to the application of Laban's principles of movement outside dance, it is noteworthy that it is usually in respect of elementary aspects such as considerations of level, size, speed and force of movement—which, however, it hardly took a Laban to point out to us. This is no accident: it is only at a low level of generality that there could be any significant application. The natural home of his "effort" and "space harmony" principles is clearly that of dance (with some aspects of "effort" having relevance also in drama and mime). To try to import them into other fields of movement practice is often to trivialise them beyond recognition, as well as to run the risk of losing sight of the particular techniques required for specific activities.

It may not be an exaggeration to suggest that the potential value of Laban's movement principles for the art of dance remains as yet barely realised. Perhaps this is inevitable as long as attempts to extend their application blurs the very domain to which they essentially belong.

## Conclusion

Laban's writings are a perpetual source of ambiguity and paradox, and those on "educational" dance are no exception. Although allowances obviously have to be made for the fact that English was not his native tongue, this is not simply a question of style. For there is more than a contingent connection between the *manner* of one's speaking and *what* is said (cf. p.8 above). As Warnock, discussing Idealist metaphysical writing, points out:-

If argument is to be carried on, rhetorical figures, stylistic variation, and literary high colour can only be distressing impediments . . . . There is an 'intrinsic' and not merely a fortuitous relation between Idealist thought and the most usual style of its expression .. . . . To strip off the highly coloured rhetorical dress would be to harm substantially the doctrine itself. (Warnock, 1958.)

Curl, referring to various translators of Laban's German works, declares that they are marked by "extravagant, florid, dogmatic and cryptic expression" (Curl, 1969), and similar characteristics in the English texts can hardly fail to be noted. Even for anyone familiar with, and perhaps having first met, Laban's ideas in practice rather than on the printed page, there remain basic difficulties and perplexities both as regards what modern educational dance is, and how it is to be justified as a curriculum activity.

On the one hand (and this is the aspect that has been seized upon by "progressive" educationists of our own day), it seems to share the ideals of the Romantic movement in art, with its glorification of experience and its ideals of self-expression, originality, communication of feeling, creative imagination, the freedom of the artist from rule and authority (the notion of mathematical proportion in art was alien to the Romantic outlook), and its comparative lack of concern with form. On the other, it owes much to Ancient Greek tradition, to which ideas of "creativity" and art as the expression of the artist's personality were wholly foreign. Indeed, there is something of a deterministic streak in Laban's thought, which stands in stark contrast to cherished notions of the freedom and independence of the individual. There are, according to the Pythagorean doctrine which Laban embraces, well-regulated, pre-established rhythms and trace-forms laid down for man to follow. He had better do so, or it will be so much the worse for him! Not only should he synchronise and attune his movement to these universal patterns for his physical and psychological well-being, but also he *ought not* to depart from these perfect, pre-ordained forms.

These two polarities can of course be reconciled by adopting a religious viewpoint—that one finds freedom and happiness when one submits to the divine will.* But this is then to confound art with religion; and when it is also mixed up with biology, physics, astronomy, and various other things, it is hardly surprising that doubts as to its logical status prevail.

Even before he turned his attention specifically to education, it seems evident that Laban viewed dance for educational purposes as somehow separable from dance as art (cf. p.98 above). But the gap between the two appears to have widened yet further with the application of his movement theories in industry—chiefly because of the development of his "effort" ideas, but also perhaps because of increasing concern with the connection between dance and social conditions of

---

* In connection with contrasts and conflicts within accounts of modern educational dance, another interesting tension arises between 'creative' dance and dance conceived of as an activity aiming at the happiness and contentment of the individual. Hudson, discussing "traditional" and "progressive" methods in education, and the possibility that the latter may in fact "withdraw . . . the cutting edge that insecurity, competition, and resentment supply," suggests that:-

> If we adjust children to themselves and each other we may remove from them the springs of their intellectual and artistic productivity. Happy children simply may not be prepared to make the effort which excellence demands. (Hudson, 1966)

living. With regard to the latter, discussion of which opens *Modern Educational Dance*, his arguments for a new form of dance are not altogether convincing. As mentioned in section 1 above, it sounds as though to be of educational value dance must be based on contemporary movement behaviour, especially working movement. "Dance movements," he (1948) says, "are basically the same as those used in everyday activities," and Modern Dance might be called "the movement expression of industrial man."

But it is not clear whether he means that dance *ought to* or actually *does* reflect, or at least is influenced by, prevailing movement characteristics of the period—in which case dance education would presumably take care of itself, and we should merely have to send children and students along to the local dance-hall once or twice a week. "Each epoch of history has its own way of dancing," he (1948) observes (and in *Mastery of Movement on the Stage* this is discussed at some length); but he goes on to maintain that "modern man has to build his own art of movement," and to this end

> Students of the contemporary forms of movement must take into consideration all shapes and rhythms which correspond to the great variety of movements developed in our industrial civilisation. (Laban, 1948.)

Either way, the reason why dance is to be regarded as educational when it shares common features with "the movement habits of modern man," and especially his "working habits," is at first obscure. Indeed the narrow range of movement of the twentieth-century industrial worker, who is engaged "in one relatively simple movement sequence which he has to perform from morning till evening throughout his lifetime," in contrast to the "rich movement life" of the craftsmen and peasants of the pre-industrial period, is deplored, and concern is expressed that

> modern working habits frequently create detrimental states of mind from which our whole civilisation is bound to suffer if no compensation is to be found. (Laban, 1948.)

Moreover, since Laban claims that this compensation is provided by the arts, dance, which is assumed to be "the basic art of man," must necessarily *contrast* with, or at least complement common movement tendencies. In this case, however, some norm is obviously presupposed which determines what the "missing" characteristics are.

Only when Laban's ideas about "effort" are grasped does it become evident why "the movements which contemporary man uses in his everyday life" are to be taken as the foundations of dance practice. This is no model for mimetic expression, a suggestion that "man at work" is to be the subject matter of dance—though this might easily be assumed by anyone reading the Introduction to *Modern Educational Dance* for the first time, and without practical experience of the subject.* Rather, working operations are seen as between them involving that variety of movement which is necessary for all-round "effort development" and "effort balance," the key to personal harmony. And because, on the one hand, actions such as digging, ironing and hammering, and, on the other, typical dance gestures such as "hitting" (cf. "battement"), "gliding" (cf. glissé) and "whipping" or "slashing" (cf. foutté) appear, when analysed in terms of force, time and space, to consist of the "same" movement elements respectively, the conclusion is drawn that practice of these common features must equip a person to cope both with his "action life," and with the world of expression and communication.

The conception of movement as a homogenous unity is thus a major error underlying the whole account of modern educational dance, though from time to time Laban gives indications that he does, in fact, sense a difference between dance movement and that of ordinary life. He recognises not only that in dance "all manner of leaps, twists, turns and other bodily movements occur, that no one would use in everyday life" (Laban, 1956), but also that as the dancer "perambulates or whirls about paths which he never would follow in his ordinary everyday occupations," his actions only *vaguely resemble* his everyday work or doings" (Laban, 1958a—my italics).

The vital significance of this distinction, however, eludes him. Because there is *some* resemblance, because in dance one is concerned with movement in a specially attentive way, he assumes that dance must be the key to success in all *doing*. For what does not involve movement? Even if one is sitting perfectly still, cogitating, weaving fancies, remembering, etc., there is still, says Laban, movement—mental movement! (cf. Essay B, part 1, above). Further, since the inner life is so intimately connected with this phenomenon (it affects our mood, reflects our emotions, feelings and indeed total personality, and is a powerful factor in interpersonal communication), what could be more important than to practise its basic elements? What could be a more worthwhile activity in education?

Such reasoning may have a simple appeal, but unfortunately is fallacious. Life would indeed be much easier if efficiency in practical tasks, "personal development," and social well-being could all be simultaneously achieved "at a stroke," as it were. But as emphasised throughout this volume, there is no uniform manifestation of such things as general skilfulness, effective communication or sensitive awareness, no one way of being imaginative, original, expressive, creative and the like. As Powell (1967) argues, intellectual and manual skills are alike context-bound and field-dependent; there are no "mysterious short cuts to wisdom" available. Or, as Hirst & Peters (1970) put it:-

---

* Only one of the sixteen themes is concerned with this, in fact—and that in relation to what are explicitly described as *primitive* working actions such as sawing, scything, etc., in order to give experience of "effort" transitions.

There are no general 'powers of the mind' that can be exercised in a vacuum. They are rather adverbial to activities and modes of experience in that they are connected with the manner in which they are conducted.

Laban, however, caught up with the notion of "effort" as an "inner impulse originating movement," seems to conceive of the mind as an entity or some kind of organ to which there is, as it were, direct access via movement, which acts upon it and thus develops personality. But as Hirst (1965) insists:-

To have a mind basically involves coming to have experience articulated by means of various conceptual schema.

It is only as finer distinctions in experience are made, so that what was once a "buzzing, booming confusion" (in William James' phrase) becomes progressively differentiated, that the growth of the mind come about. Contrary to what might at first seem to be the case, the making of distinctions (which is not to be confused with rigid separating) leads not to disintegration, but to ever greater comprehension, a grasping of complexities through a developing awareness of the differences, but at the same time the similarities and connections, between their various aspects.

Movement experience, therefore, once a global affair, becomes increasingly diversified as different ways of directing and organising it are developed according to the particular purposes which it may serve. One such mode of experience is that which involves attending to structured movement forms as objects of *aesthetic contemplation,* i.e. without consideration of any further function which they might fulfil. This special kind of "disinterested" attending and contemplating an object as a thing in its own right, and not as instrumental to some further end, calls for concentration on its *formal* properties, on just what it consists of, and not for considerations of its practical or utilitarian implications. And movement artefacts whose formal properties are of intrinsic significance, and so command this kind of attention, are what we know as *dances.*

Though in the past these often came into being because of social, religious, magic and other purposes, and continued for long years to be regarded primarily as vehicles of extra-aesthetic values, it would seem that an aesthetic motive was also frequently operative, that the aesthetic impulse is indeed manifest throughout history, but was not consciously recognised (cf. Osborne, 1968). In fact what had been at work in the creation and enjoyment of art of all kinds began to be appreciated for what it was only comparatively recently. It is only with the evolution of the concept of "disinterestedness" in art in the eighteenth century that the aesthetic consciousness shows signs of emerging in the West. Previously, interest had centred almost exclusively on the *uses* of art—on its moral and social effects, on its powers of evoking emotion, and so on. The idea of art existing solely, or at least primarily, for aesthetic contemplation was totally unknown in classical antiquity, the Middle Ages and the Renaissance period alike.

The significance of this attitude, which amounts to a new aspect of the development of mind, an extending of the powers of perception and of our "commerce with the world" (in Osborne's phrase), can hardly be overestimated:-

> What happened was something more than just a new theory or a new twist to theoretical habits. It was more akin to the discovery of a new dimension of self-consciousness . . . (Osborne, 1968.)

But the nature of such experience seems frequently to be misunderstood among proponents of modern educational dance, and terms such as "disinterestedness," "contemplation," "detachment," and "distance," in the aesthetic sense, misinterpreted. "Disinterested" does not, of course, imply "*un*interested." It stands in opposition to attitudes of *self-interest,* as when engaging in an activity such as dancing, painting a picture, reading poetry or listening to music, for reasons of utility, e.g. emotional relief, or social advantage—with *manipulating* or using it for extraneous purposes. To turn again to Osborne (1968):-

> Our interest, if it is an aesthetic interest, 'terminates' in the object and we are wholly engrossed in perceiving, contemplating and perfecting our awareness of the object upon which our attention is directed. *

Nor does "disinterested" or "detached" refer to aloofness or absence of feeling. On the contrary, aesthetic experience is often highly charged with feeling of a particular kind, and involves a special sort of personal involvement and commitment, both on the part of the artist and of the spectator or listener, as well as the performer in the case of dance, drama and music (cf. Osborne's "wholly engrossed" above). But this is only possible through a *distancing* from the interests and urgencies of everyday life (the yokel who rushes onto the stage to "save" the hapless heroine has not achieved this, cf. Bullough, 1912). Similarly, "contemplation" is not a matter of passivity, and applies not only to the audience but to the performer. Reid (1970) makes the penetrating observation:-

> Even when we are quietly sitting or standing still, a great deal may be going on: and a dancer or actor . . . is often, perhaps always, in some degree contemplating the product of his own activity. In playing a musical instrument it is very important to *listen* to one's own playing.

---

* This is precisely what those who speak of "movement experience" and "knowing movement" would seem to be talking about—but it goes unrecognised for what it is. Similarly, references to the *meaning* of movement in modern educational dance literature make most sense when taken as *aesthetic* meaning.

It is not altogether surprising that Laban, more influenced it would seem by ancient Greek thought than by aesthetic debate of his own day, was unfamiliar with the concept of the aesthetic in modern terms, and though obviously aware of a difference between movement engaged in "for itself" and for utilitarian purposes,* nevertheless adopts a thoroughly instrumental attitude towards art. Rather than regarding dance as a self-rewarding activity, he consistently views it as a means to some further end—a means of establishing psychological equilibrium, of promoting group harmony, of "producing moments of ecstasy or clairvoyant concentration" (Laban, 1966), and so on.

Such non-aesthetic considerations still tend to dominate present-day attitudes to "educational" dance, and nothing is more ironic than the fact that while Laban's categorisation of movement provides the very means whereby dances may be created and assessed by formalistic criteria of their own, and need no longer be dependent on external standards applicable to other activities, concern is still largely with dance as a mirror or an instrument—a mirror of some aspect of reality outside movement itself, an instrument for the achievement of a variety of benefits. When, moreover, the Classical version of instrumentalist theory is allied with that of the Romantic, it is perhaps not to be wondered at that in education less seems to be heard of dance in aesthetic terms, than in connection with personal satisfaction, emotional experience, moral awareness, social cohesion, interpersonal understanding, relief from academic pressure, and the like.† *Of course* such things are important, and that dance *may* have such valuable "spin-offs" is a happy coincidence. And, as argued in section 3, some of these considerations might have to be taken into account as "latent objectives" in weighing the various merits of various curriculum activities. But they neither define what dance as an educational activity is, nor must they be allowed to dominate procedure in the teaching of it.

In any case, it seems inevitable that enormous personal gain must result from each "raid on the inarticulate" (in T.S. Eliot's phrase), or, in Bantock's (1967) words, the "perpetually renewed, demonic, immensely joyous struggle with intractable material and media" that typifies artistic endeavour. But it is clear that "creative" dance cannot be the complete account of dance in education. It is not only that there is room for study of particular dance styles as part of the history of dance, but models both for performance and appreciation are necessary for, and not antipathetic to, the achieving of ultimate freedom and independence in the dance. Furthermore, though their beginnings may be lost in the mist of time, and their

---

* The dancer's actions "are never really purposeful in the ordinary sense of utility." (Laban, 1958a).

† One would not have to be a reckless gambler to wager that students of dance in colleges of education would be likely to reveal far greater knowledge of such things as dance as a social force, as religion, as magic, as allied with drama, etc. than of dance as an art form in its own right. Interesting and fascinating as these may be, if central aesthetic concepts remain unexamined, there would seem to be a serious lack of balance here.

original significance no longer relevant today, they may be studied now from a conscious aesthetic standpoint. To this end, as already suggested, Laban's movement classification is of direct value.

Finally, in striving both to establish a secure place for dance in education and to continue to improve existing standards, we might do well as educators to seek to cultivate that manner of approaching problems, particularly those deriving from former influential minds, which McKellar (1957) describes. Prefacing his chapter on "Conditions of Creativity" with Poincaré's dictum that "to doubt everything or to believe everything are two equally convenient solutions; both dispense with the necessity of reflection," he goes on to suggest:-

> The attitude that appears most readily to favour creative thinking combines receptivity towards what is valuable, in traditional and new ideas alike, with discriminating criticisms of both. A thinker on these lines is uninterested in established ideas when they are obviously wrong—this is the preserve of the destructive critic. He is concerned, rather, with vigorously criticising ideas, both new and old, where they are most nearly right. To employ a mental model which may perhaps be appropriate, he is more concerned with 'growing points' than with 'dead wood'.

It is high time that the "dead wood" was cut out of modern educational dance theory, and the "growing points" detected and carefully nurtured. There is so much "nearly right" in Laban (as well as, of course, much that is absolutely right), and this we have to try to unravel and reconstruct. Though the term "movement education" may ultimately be found to be inadequate, we cannot but agree with Curl (1969) that:-

> Whatever Laban's fundamental philosophy . . . the fact remains that he has initiated both a new attitude to Movement Education in this country and a new method of teaching, from which we have reaped rich rewards.

References

ADAMS M. (1969) The concept of physical education—II. In Proceedings of the Annual Conference, Phil. Educ. Soc. G.B.
BANTOCK G.H. (1967) "Education, Culture and the Emotions". London: Faber.
BEDFORD E. (1965) Emotions. In D.F. Gustafson (Ed.) "Essays in Philosophical Psychology". London: Macmillan.
BLACKIE J. (1967) "Inside the Primary School". London: H.M.S.O.
BUBER M. (1961) "Between Man and Man". London: Fontana.
BULLOUGH E. (1912) 'Psychical distance' as a factor in art and an aesthetic principle. Republished (1960) in M. Rader (Ed) "A Modern Book of Aesthetics." (3rd. edit.) New York: Holt, Rinehart & Winston.
CARROLL J. & LOFTHOUSE P. (1969) "Creative Dance for Boys". London: Macdonald & Evans.
CASEY J. (1966) "The Language of Criticism". London: Methuen.
CHARLTON W. (1970) "Aesthetics". London: Hutchinson.
CLARK SIR K. (1956) "The Nude". London: Murray.
COHEN S.J. (1966) "The Modern Dance: seven statements of belief". Connecticut: Wesleyan Univ. Press
CURL G.F. (1966) Philosophic foundations (Part 1). *L.A.M.G.Mag.,* **37,** 7-15.
CURL G.F. (1967a) Philosophic foundations (Part 2). *L.A.M.G.Mag.,* **38,** 7-17.
CURL G.F. (1967b) Philosophic foundations (Part 3). *L.A.M.G.Mag.,* **39,** 25-34.
CURL G.F. (1968a) Philosophic foundations (Part 4). *L.A.M.G.Mag.,* **40,** 27-37.
CURL G.F. (1968b) Philosophic foundations (Part 5). *L.A.M.G.Mag.,* **41,** 23-29.
CURL G.F. (1969) Philosophic foundations (Part 6). *L.A.M.G.Mag.,* **43,** 27-44.
DEARDEN R.F. (1968) "The Philosophy of Primary Education". London: Routledge & Kegan Paul.
DEWEY J. (1934) "Art as Experience". New York: Capricorn.
DOWNIE R.S. & TELFER E. (1969) "Respect for Persons". London: Allen & Unwin.
DUNCAN I. (1927) "My Life" Republished (1955). New York: Liverwright Pub. Corp.
††FINDLAY J.N. (1967) The perspicuous and the poignant. *Brit. J. Aesthet.* **7,** 3-19
GOODRICH J. (1956) The Laban Art of Movement Centre *L.A.M.G. Mag.* 17,7-10
GOTTLIEB G. (1968) "The Logic of Choice". London: Allen & Unwin.
GREGER S. (1968) Presentational theories need unpacking. *Brit. J. Aesthet.* **9,** 157-170.
††HEPBURN R. (1961) Emotions and emotional qualities. *Brit. J. Aesthet.* **1,** 255-265.
HIRST P.H. (1965) Liberal education and the nature of knowledge. In R.D. Archambault (Ed.) "Philosophical Analysis and Education". London: Routledge & Kegan Paul.

---

†† These papers are also in H. Osborne (Ed.) "Aesthetics in the Modern World." London: Thames & Hudson (1968).

HIRST P.H. & PETERS R.S. (1970) "The Logic of Education". London: Routledge & Kegan Paul.

HOSPERS J. (1946) "Meaning and Truth in the Arts". Chapel Hill: Univ. of N. Carolina Press.

HUDSON L. (1966) "Contrary Imaginations". London: Methuen.

KENNY A. (1963) "Action, Emotion and Will". London: Routledge & Kegan Paul.

LABAN R. & LAWRENCE F.C. (1947) "Effort". London: Macdonald & Evans.

LABAN R. (1948) "Modern Educational Dance". London: Macdonald & Evans.

LABAN R. (1950) "Mastery of Movement on the Stage". London: Macdonald & Evans.

LABAN R. (1952) The art of movement in the school. *L.A.M.G.Mag.,* **8,** 10-16.

LABAN R. (1954) The work of the Art of Movement Studio. *J. Phys. Ed.* **46,** 23-30

LABAN R. (1955) From Rudolf Laban's early writings. *L.A.M.G.Mag.,* **15,** 12-23.

LABAN R. (1956) "Principles of Dance and Movement Notation". London: Macdonald & Evans.

*LABAN R. (1957) Education through the arts. *L.A.M.G.Mag.,* **19,** 4-7.

*LABAN R. (1958a) The world of rhythm and harmony. *L.A.M.G.Mag.,* **20,** 6-9.

*LABAN R. (1958b) Movement concerns the whole man. *L.A.M.G.Mag.,* **21,** 9-13.

*LABAN R. (1959a) Dance as a discipline. *L.A.M.G.Mag.,* **22,** 33-39.

*LABAN R. (1959b) Meaning. *L.A.M.G.Mag.,* **22,** 22-24.

*LABAN R. (1959c) The importance of dancing. *L.A.M.G.Mag.,* **22,** 5-17.

LABAN R. (1959d) The rhythm of living energy. *L.A.M.G.Mag.,* **22,** 40-47.

LABAN R. (1960) "The Mastery of Movement" (2nd. edit. revised L. Ullmann). London: Macdonald & Evans.

*LABAN R. (1961) Dance in general. *L.A.M.G.Mag.,* **26,** 11-24.

LABAN R. (1963) "Modern Educational Dance" (2nd. edit. revised L. Ullmann). London: Macdonald & Evans.

LABAN R. (1966) "Choreutics" (Ed. L. Ullmann). London: Macdonald & Evans.

LANGER S.K. (1942) "Philosophy in a New Key". Cambridge (Mass.): Harvard Univ. Press.

LANGER S.K. (1953) "Feeling and Form". London: Routledge & Kegan Paul.

LANGFORD G. (1968) "Philosophy and Education". London: Macmillan.

LAYSON J.E. (1970) The contribution of modern dance to education. Unpublished M. Ed. dissertation Univ. Manchester.

MACDONALD M. (1951) Review article. *Mind,* **60,** 561-564.

MACMURRAY J. (1957) "Persons in Relation". London: Faber.

MARTIN J. (1933) "The Modern Dance" (Republished 1965). New York: Dance Horizons.

MCKELLAR P. (1957) "Imagination and Thinking". London: Cohen & West.

MEAD G.H. (1934) "Mind, Self and Society". Chicago: Univ. Press.

††MORRIS-JONES H. (1962) The language of feelings. *Brit. J. Aesthet.* **2,** 17-25.

---

* These papers are also in L. Ullman (Ed) "Rudolph Laban Speaks about Movement and Dance." Surrey: Lisa Ullman (1971).

NORTH M. (1971) But where is the movement? A critique. *Univ. London Inst. Educ. Bull.,* **23,** Spring.

OAKESHOTT M. (1962a) The voice of poetry in the conversation of mankind. In "Rationalism in Politics and Other Essays". London: Methuen.

OAKESHOTT M. (1962b) Political education. In "Rationalism in Politics and Other Essays". London: Methuen.

OAKESHOTT M. (1967) Learning and teaching. In R.S. Peters (Ed.) "The Concept of Education". London: Routledge & Kegan Paul.

††OSBORNE H. (1963) The quality of feeling in art. *Brit. J. Aesthet.* **3,** 38-53.

OSBORNE H. (1968) "Aesthetics and Art Theory: an historical introduction". London: Longmans.

PETERS R.S. (1961) Emotions and the category of passivity. *Proc. Arist. Soc.,* **LXII,** 117-42.

PETERS R.S. (1965) Education as initiation. In R.D. Archambault (Ed.) "Philosophical Analysis and Education". London: Routledge & Kegan Paul.

PETERS R.S. (1966) "Ethics and Education". London: Allen & Unwin.

PHENIX P.H. (1964) "Realms of Meaning". New York: McGraw Hill.

POLANYI M. (1958) "Personal Knowledge". London: Routledge & Kegan Paul.

POWELL J. (1967) On learning to be original, witty, flexible, resourceful, etc. Proceedings of the Annual Conference, Phil. Educ. Soc. G.B.

PRALL D.W. (1936) "Aesthetic Analysis". New York: Crowell.

PRESTON-DUNLOP V. (1963) "A Handbook for Modern Educational Dance". London: Macdonald & Evans.

REDFERN H.B. (1963) "Introducing Laban Art of Movement". London: Macdonald & Evans.

REID L.A. (1957) The philosophy of education through the arts. Report of the Conference of the Joint Council for Education through Art.

REID L.A. (1961) "Ways of Knowledge and Experience". London: Allen & Unwin.

REID L.A. (1969) "Meaning in the Arts". London: Allen & Unwin.

REID L.A. (1970) Movement and meaning. *L.A.M.G.Mag.,* **45,** 5-31.

RUSSELL J. (1958) "Modern Dance in Education". London: Macdonald & Evans.

RUSSELL J. (1965) "Creative Dance in the Primary School". London: Macdonald & Evans.

RUSSELL J. (1969) "Creative Dance in the Secondary School". London: Macdonald & Evans.

RYLE G. (1949) "The Concept of Mind". London: Hutchinson.

SACHS C. (1937) "World History of the Dance". New York: Norton.

SCHEFFLER I. (1965) "Conditions of Knowledge". Glenview: Scott Foresman.

SELDEN E. (1930) "Elements of the Free Dance". New York: Barnes.

SHAFFER J.A. (1968) "Philosophy of Mind". London: Prentice Hall.

SHEETS M. (1966) "The Phenomenology of Dance". Madison: Univ. of Wisconsin Press.

STEVENSON C.L. (1944) "Ethics and Language". New Haven: Yale Univ. Press.

ULLMANN L. (1960) Movement education. *L.A.M.G.Mag.,* **24,** 19-28.

WARNOCK G.J. (1958) "English Philosophy since 1900". Oxford: Univ. Press.

146

WEITZ M. (1962) The role of theory in aesthetics. In J. Margolis (Ed.) "Philosophy Looks at the Arts". New York: Scribners.

WIGMAN M. (1959) The extraordinary thing Laban gave to the dance. *The New Era,* **40,** 102-103.

WIGMAN M. (1966) "The Language of Dance". London: Macdonald & Evans.

WITTGENSTEIN L. (1953) "Philosophical Investigations". Oxford: Blackwell.

WOLLHEIM R. (1968) "Art and Its Objects". London: Harper & Row.

WOLLHEIM R. (1971) Talking about aesthetics. *The Listener,* **85,** 201-204.

# INDEX OF PROPER NAMES

Adams, M., 113, 121
Ayer, A.J., 44

Bantock, G.H., 48, 79, 80, 95, 141
Beardsley, M., 38
Bedford, E., 90
Berkeley, G., 32
Best, G., 10
Blackie, J., 134
Buber, M., 108
Bullough, E., 12, 77n, 140

Caesar, J., 11
Carlisle, R., 41, 118
Carroll, J., 123n
Casey, J., 74
Charlton, W., 74, 94n, 110, 125, 126
Clark, Sir K., 128
Cohen, S.J., 82
Coleridge, S.T., 18, 92
Curl, G.F., ix, 44, 97, 99, 100, 118,
    119, 122, 125, 127, 133, 134,
    136, 142

Dearden, R.F., 44, 48n, 50n
Descartes, R., 28, 37
Dewey, J., 18, 73
Dilman, I., 15
Downie, R.S., 97n
Duncan, I., 62, 66, 73, 85

Eliot, T.S., 133, 141
Findlay, J.N., 74
Flew, A., 4, 6, 8
Freud, S., x, 36
Furlong, E.J., 4, 7, 13

George IV, 11
Goodrich, J., 120
Gottleib, G., 120
Graham, M., 18, 73, 75, 80n, 81, 103
Greger, S., 126
Griffiths, A.P., 43n

Hepburn, R., 94n
Hepton, B., 39n
Hirst, P.H., xn, 2, 21, 52, 78, 99, 108
    109, 110, 111, 138, 139
Hitler, A., 4
Hospers, J., 18, 34n, 73
Hudson, L., 1, 14, 136n
Humphrey, D., 82

Ishiguro, H., 19

Jahoda, M., 47
James, W., 139
Jooss, K., 74

Kennedy, D., 15
Kennedy, J., 10
Kenny, A., 90, 91

Laban, R., viii, ix-xii, 8, 17, 20, Essays
    B, C, *passim*
Langer, S.K., 10, 38, 72, 73, 74, 77n,
    78, 81, 109, 112, 133
Langford, G., 62n
Lawrence, F.C., 25, 30, 36, 116
Lawrie, J., 12
Layson, J., 62n
Lofthouse, P., 123n
Loren, S., 109

148

Macdonald, M., 126
MacIntyre, A.C., x
Macmurray, J., 108
Martin, J., 81
McKellar, P., 6n, 21, 142
Mead, G.H., 10, 112
Melden, A.I., 43n
Menuhin, Y., 4
Mill, J.S., 48
Moffo, A., 12
Morris-Jones, H., 94n
Mozart, W.A., 8

Nelson, H., 4
Newton, Sir I., 4, 119
North, M., 134
Noverre, J.G., 85

Oakeshott, M., 19, 20, 21, 78, 82, 98,
    109n, 131
O'Connor, D.J., ix, xi
Osborne, H., 74, 81, 82, 84, 92, 93,
    94, 95, 101, 126, 139, 140

Peters, R.S., xn, 1, 2, 21, 42, 48, 62n,
    90, 91, 97n, 108, 109, 110, 111,
    112, 113, 138
Phenix, P.H., 78, 112
Plato, 47
Plowright, J., 39n
Poincarè, M., 142
Polanyi, M., 108
Powell, J., 132, 138
Prall, D.W., 124
Preston-Dunlop, V., 16n, 68, 103,
    104, 107, 123, 124

Redfern, H.B., 107
Reid, L.A., 38n, 48, 54, 74, 78, 83,
    94n, 108, 112, 113, 140
Rousseau, J.J., 54
Russell, J., 14, 123n
Ryle, G., xii, 6, 12, 13, 28, 133

Sachs, G., 54, 66, 92n, 96, 97, 100,
    131
Scheffler, I., 132
Selden, E., 125
Shaffer, J.A ., 34n, 91n
Sheets, M., 114
Sobers, G., 4
Socrates, ix, 48
Spinoza, B., 50
St. Denis, R., 62
Stephenson, G., 39n
Stevenson, C.L., 134n

Taylor, P., 4
Telfer, E., 97n

Ullmann, L., 14, 25, 31, 49, 63, 117,
    123, 131

Vesey, G., 43n

Warnock, G.J., 135
Weitz, M., 85
White, A.R., 43n
White, J.P., 15
Wigman, M., 73, 129, 130
Wittgenstein, L., vii, 2, 3, 78, 91, 120n
Wollheim, R., 20, 38, 52, 53, 77, 94n,
95n

# SUBJECT INDEX

Absorption, 12, 96
Achievements, 95-98, 102, 103
Acting, 5, 6, 7, 10, 12-13, 36
Action(s), 43-44, 52, 72, 76, 89-90,
    92, 100, 101, 138
    "action-moods," 76, 79, 94
    "action-training," 42-44
    reflex, 34, 43
Activity, activities, 11, 26, 27, 28, 34,
    43-44, 50n, 72, 125, 133
Actors, 12, 46, 69, 134
Aesthetic(s) 38, 52, 53, 54, 78, 94, 99,
    101, 116, 139-142
    appreciation, 18-20
    contemplation, 18, 139-140
    detachment, 91, 140
    education, 19, 57, 63
    form of understanding (mode of
        experience), x, 11, 21, 63, 79,
        103, 105, 107, 114, 122, 139
    pleasure, 49, 76, 125
    value (merit), 15, 17, 83, 129
Aim(s), 14, 26, 61, 68, 75, 81, 82, 85,
    89, 96, 101, 105, 113, 134
Art, 15-16, 20, 51-55, Essay C passim
"Art of movement," vii, viii, ix, xi, 43,
    48, 57, 65, 99, 117, 132, 133, 137
"Attitude of the other," 10, 112

"Basic movement," 134
Believing falsely (mistakenly), 5, 6,
    11-12
Body-mind relationship, 32-35, 39,
    68, 88

Catharsis, 11, 76, 79
"Choreutic(s)," 26, 124, 126, 127,
    128
Classical ballet, 18, 66, 82, 103, 125,
    129
Communication, 8-9, 70, 71, 80-81,
    83, 87, 99, 102, 105, 107, 109-111,
    114-116, 136, 138
    non-verbal, xn, 36, 39, 69
    powers of ("capacity to comm-
        unicate"), 42, 99, 115
    theory of art, 52, 80, 109
"Creative"
    activity, activities, 14, 63, 68,
        80, 81, 87, 96
    dance, vii, 3, 14, 21, 71, 75, 81,
        86, 116, 131, 136n, 141
    expression, 64, 71-86
Creativity (creativeness), 1, 3, 13-16,
    71, 132, 136
Curriculum construction (planning),
    ix, 62

Dance,
    appreciation, 18-21, 67, 86, 123,
        129, 131, 141
    composing, composition(s), 7,
        15, 16-17, 49, 56, 67, 81, 86,
        Essay C, section 4 passim
    -drama, 85, 111
    folk-, 54, 85
    "free," 63, 65-70, 81
    -image, 38, 75

Modern, 62-68, 73-74, 81, 104, 123
    modern educational, viii, 1, 3, 17-18, 20, 35, 43, 56-57, Essay C
    national, 53, 77
    notation, 8, 123
    presentation, 102-103
Daydreaming, 4, 5, 6, 7
"Disinterestedness," 139-140
"Distance, "distancing," 12, 140
"Double aspect" theory of mind, 32-33
Drama, 3, 10, 11, 13, 14, 20, 39, 43, 46, 56, 75, 81, 84, 102, 107, 108, 111, 116n, 135, 140, 141n
Dualism, 32-33, 34, 88

Ecstasy, 96-97, 100-101, 105, 141
Education, x, xi, 1, 5, 12, 13, 17, 20, 33, 39, 40, 43, 47, 49, 52, 53-56, Essay C passim
    moral, 9
    physical, ix, 9, 20, 38, 41, 43, 66, 113, 116n, 128, 135
    theory of, vii
"Effort(s)," 3, Essay B passim, 61, 66, 68, 76, 78, 87, 88, 89, 91, 98, Essay C: section 4 passim
    —action(s), 29, 30-31, 42, 76, 88
    —balance, 40, 45-49, 56, 68, 76, 123, 138
    —development, 40, 49-55, 56, 68, 138
    —elements, 29, 30, 46, 56, 68, 94, 95, 124
    —harmony, 40, 56, 76, 93n, 123
    incomplete, 44
    mental, 28, 34, 35-36
    —training, 40, 41-45, 51, 55-56, 68, 84, 117
Emotions, 11, 14, 33, 48, 67, 71-86, 90-94, 101, 106, 109, 138, 139

Empathising, 5, 6, 9-11
Energy, 27, 29, 30, 34, 56, 73, 124, 125
"Eukinetics,," 25, 40
Exertion, 25, 28, 30, 33
Experience, 63, 64, 81, Essay C: section 2b passim 129, 136
    life—, 81-82, 84, 86
    movement—, 84, 134, 135, 139, 140n
    private, 8, 16, 102, 129
Expression, 1, 10, 14, 20, 37, 39, 52, 56, 64, 68, Essay C: sections 2a, 2b passim, 106, 109, 114-115, 136, 137
    self—, 11, 71, 73, 75, 80, 81-84, 136
Expressionist theories of art, 52, 74, 85, 87, 109, 125, 126
"Expressive" aspects of modern educational dance, 63, 64, 68, Essay C: section 2a

Faculty psychology, 3, 14, 41
"Family resemblance," 2
"Feeling(s), " 1, 11, 14, 17, 20, 34, 39, 48, 52, Essay C: sections 2a, 2b passim, 109, 110, 136, 138, 140
Flow, 29, 31, 46, 50, 65, 66, 68, 97, 99, 101, 105-106, 123, 124
Force, 30, 135, 138
Formal aspects, properties of movement, 76, 84-85, 125, 129, 139, 140
Formalist theories of art, 85
Freedom, 65, 88, 128, 131, 134, 136, 141

Games, 10, 107, 111, 112, 113
"Ghost in the machine," 28, 33
Golden Section, 126
Group
    dance, 48n, 64, 105, 114

interplay (*see also* Social aspects of modern educational dance), 10

"Growth" theory, 49-50

Happiness, 45, 48, 136n
Harmonisation, 47-48, 106, 118, 122, 124
Harmony, 25, 47, 49, 53, 54, 97, 99, 100, 105-106, 114, 120-124, 127, 138, 141
Health, 48
History, 4, 111, 112
    of dance, 141

Identity theory of mind, 32, 34, 39
Imagination, Essay A, 42, 71, 111, 115
    creative, 5, 6, 13-21, 81, 99, 136
    movement—, 17
Imaging, 5, 6-9, 21
Imitation, imitating, 10, 12, 13, 14
"Impressive" aspects of movement, 64, 79, Essay C: section 2b, 122
"Inner attitude," 30, 31, 34, 68, 76
Integration (*see also* "Wholeness"), 47-48, 100
Intention(s), 15, 26, 30, 34, 43, 48, 50n, 52, 54, 71-72, 89, 101, 111, 134
Interactionism, 33

"Kinesphere," 26, 120, 124, 127
Kinetic ideas (*see also* Movement ideas), 17, 66, 68, 84, 131
Kinetography Laban, 16
Knowledge, ix, 12-13, 17, 20, 62, 64, 67, 82, 88, 98, 111-114, 131, 132, 133
    self—, 55, 69, 112

Latent objectives, 113, 114, 116, 141

Language, 2, 3, 13, 26, 27, 43, 52, 61, 72, 82, 131
"Language of dance," 69, 73, 129, 131
"Language games," 78, 133
Laws of movement, 99, 119-122
Learning, 11, 21, 53, 55, 56, 98
Linguistic usage, 2, 6, 27
Literature, 3, 20, 61, 82, 111
Make-believe, 5, 12
Meaning(s), ix, xi, 2, 3, 52, 77, 85, 89, 90, 118, 129, 140n
Mental,
    activity, activities, 34-36
    events, 32, 37, 88
    experience, 16, 39, 52
    faculty, faculties, 3, 28, 41, 48, 90-91
    function(s), 3, 31, 32
    health, 48
    illness, 46-47
    images, imagery, 4, 6-9, 16
    qualities, 99
Mime, (mimetic), 36, 39, 52, 56, 84, 135, 137
Mimicking (*see also* Imitation), 13
Mind, 28, 32-35, 53, 98, 99, 127, 139
    development of, 53, 100, 139, 140
    "impact of movement on," 64, Essay C: section 2b, 118
    "powers of," 139
Modes (forms) of experience, understanding, xn, 20, 62, 63, 98, 139
Mood(s), 11, 30, 33, 48, Essay C: sections 2a, 2b *passim*, 114, 117 138
Motif-writing, 16
Motor ability factor, 41, 55, 69
Movement,
    education, x, 11, 54, 142
    elements, 19, 25, 29, 37, 38-39,

44, 55, 63, 67-68, 76, 77, 84,
85, 88, 93, 95, 102, 114, 123,
130, 138
ideas (*see also* Kinetic ideas),
123, 126
notation (*see also* Dance
notation), 8
observation, 11, 69-70, 116
principles, 64, 67, 87, 104, Essay
C: section 4
research, 64, 87, 117-118
scale(s), 103, 124. 126
themes, 76, 97, 118, 122, 130,
138n
—thinking, 51-52
Music, 3, 7, 8, 9, 15, 20, 49, 61, 66,
67, 74, 82, 102, Essay C: section 4
*passim*
Myth, 119, 133

Nature, 53, 56

Orientation, 120, 124
Originality, 5, 13, 14, 15, 16, 18, 81,
132, 136

Painting(s), 3, 9, 20, 54, 61, 69, 81, 84
Panpsychism, 29
Pattern(s), 7, 67, 69, 75, 85, 122, 124,
125, 130
Perception(s), 18-19, 88, 101, 140
Perceptual qualities, 38
Personal interaction (*see also* Communication), 69, 116
Personality,
assessment, xn, 36
creative activity and expression
of, 81-84
development of, 98, 102, 128,
139
effect of dance and movement
on, 63, Essay C: section 2c
integration ("harmonisation")

of, 47, 48, Essay C: section 2c
movement as a reflection of, 44,
46, 69, 114, 138
Philosophy, viii, ix, xi, 1, 2, 4, 118
of mind, 53, 90
Physical behaviour, 8, 9, 38, 43, 44,
46, 72
Play, 55, 78, 98, 99, 112
Plowden Report, 135
Poetry, 20, 74, 81, 82, 102, 128, 130,
140
Pretending (*see also* Acting), 12
Proportion(s), 126-127, 134, 136

Reality (real life), 7, 12, 77, 92-93,
107-112, 115, 116
non—, 6, 10, 93
Recovery, 27, 46, 49, 56
Recreation, 97, 98, 100
Relationships, 11, 64, Essay C:
section 3 *passim,* 130
Relaxation, 35, 124
Representational,
movement, 7, 84
theory of art, 85, 126
"Respect for persons," 97
Rhythm(s), rhythmic movement, 7, 8,
28, 30, 39, 46, 55, 56, 67, 69, 77, 78,
84, 89, 94, 99, 104, Essay C:
section 4 *passim*
Romanticism, 74, 81, 84, 136
Rule(s), 33, 119-122, 128, 136

Sculpture, 9, 61
"Shadow-movements," x, 10, 36-37,
115
Shape(s), 7, 55, 78, 89, 104, 115, 123,
124. 125, 130, 137
Skilfulness, Essay B: part 2 *passim,*
69, 115, 138
Skill(s), 17-19, 27, 39, Essay B: part 2
*passim,* 62, 69, 82, 129n, 131, 132,
133

Social aspects of modern educational
   dance, 81, Essay C: section 3
Socialisation, 62
"Space harmony," 7, 25, 44, 75, 97,
   123-125, 128, 135
Spontaneity, 1, 14-15, 55, 83, 88,
   106, 128, 134
State(s) of mind, 9, 39, 42, 51, 53, 55,
   72-79, 87-102, 122, 137
Style(s), 63, 65-68, 81, 82, 103-104,
   117, 130, 131, 132, 141
Symbol(s), symbolising, 8-9, 20, 52,
   77
Sympathy, 9, 13

T'ai Ch'i Ch'uan, 48
*Techne,* 119, 131
Technique(s), 9, 16, 18, 20, 21, 53,
   55, 68, 98, 103, 119, 128, 131,
   132, 133, 134, 135
Therapy, 62, 80, 97
Thinking, 3, 13, 21, 34, 35, 39, 42, 48,
   52, 96, 99, 100
Thought(s), 20, 71, 79, 90, 100, 110
"Trace-forms," 99, 124, 136
Training, 18, 39, 42, 55, 134

Understanding, 17, 56, 98, 102, 115
      moral, 113
      movement, 56, 115, 134
      interpersonal, xn, 39, 69, 79,
         111-116, 141
      personal (*see also* Knowledge of
         self), xn, 39, 79, 113
Unity, 95, 97, 98, 100, 101, 105, 123,
   124, 126
      organic, 126

"Wholeness," (*see also* "Integration"),
   47, 83
Work, working movement, 41-42, 45,
   50, 65, 69, 78, 93, 133, 137, 138